God Images
and Self Esteem

God Images and Self Esteem

Empowering Women in a Patriarchal Society

Carroll Saussy

Westminster/John Knox Press
Louisville, Kentucky

Scripture quotations are from *The Jerusalem Bible,* copyright © 1966, 1967, 1968 by Darton, Longman & Todd, Ltd., and Doubleday & Co., Inc. Used by permission of the publishers.

Book design by Ken Taylor

First edition

Published by Westminster/John Knox Press
Louisville, Kentucky

PRINTED IN THE UNITED STATES OF AMERICA

9   8   7   6   5   4   3   2   1

Library of Congress Cataloging-in-Publication Data

Saussy, Carroll.
  God images and self esteem : empowering women in a patriarchal society / Carroll Saussy. — 1st ed.
      p.   cm.
  Includes bibliographical references and index.
  ISBN 0-664-25199-4

  1. Women—Religious life. 2. Self-respect in women. 3. Feminism—Religious aspects—Christianity. 4. Self-respect—Religious aspects—Christianity. I. Title.
BV4527.S28   1991
208′.2—dc20   91-3482

L

For my nieces and grandnieces, sixty in number and growing, that they may know and rejoice in their true selves.

For women colleagues and students who convinced me that this book was to be written.

For Frank, who continues to love me into the fullness of life.

Acknowledgments

Many people strengthened my resolve to write this book. Others engaged with me when the book was underway. I am grateful to them all. Emma Justes, a member of the steering committee of the Society for Pastoral Theology, invited me to present a "work in progress" at that group's annual meeting in Denver in June of 1989. Although I had barely moved toward a manuscript at that time, I accepted the invitation with the proviso that Emma be part of my presentation. Emma, Carolyn Bohler, and Shelley Finson—wonderful sisters—graciously became a weave of women with me as we talked through what I wanted to present and where they would engage in the discussion. If it were not for the society and for the response I received at that session, the book as written surely would not exist. The advice and encouragement I received was just the motivation I needed to see the task through.

When the group gathered for the plenary session at the Brown Palace Hotel, I asked the women to sit in an inner circle, the men in the outer circle, so that each group might speak in turn out of its own experience—the women going first because women's self-understanding was central to my study. As people began shifting seats, I heard a male voice behind me grumble, "I wonder if this is far enough back for her." Indeed, I had overstepped my bounds from the perspective of some of the men in attendance. However, the Society for Pastoral Theology is centrally committed to being an egalitarian society, and at the 1990 meeting heated gender issues left unresolved from the previous gathering were worked through, the inner circle of women focused on feminist issues being but one of them. I believe the Society for Pastoral Theology emerged stronger and more credible because of the confrontation. I am deeply grateful for that hopeful society, which witnesses to new possibilities for women and men working together as equals.

I am indebted to the twenty-one women who volunteered to be a part of the research that supports this book. They were wonderfully inspiring teachers. For reading and commenting on early drafts of the manuscripts, I thank Jane Schaberg, Mary Hunt, Ruth Duba, Bob Wicks, Charles Stewart, and my best critic, Frank Molony. For splendid sisterly support, I thank my colleagues Denise Hopkins and Gail Unterberger. For the many ways in which she was an invaluable assistant, I thank my student and colleague Betsy Halsey. For coming to my rescue when computer or printer lost its memory, I thank my niece Suzanne Saussy Parker. For his encouragement from the first day we met and discussed my work, I thank my editor, Harold Twiss. Finally, I am grateful to Wesley Theological Seminary for a sabbatical that set me free to do the work.

C. S.

Contents

Introduction

Faith and Self Esteem

My interest in both religious faith and self esteem grew out of my own journey, and most significantly out of my family of origin. The fifth of eight children, I grew up in a generally tumultuous and often conflicted family who lived in a large, sometimes chaotic house in New Orleans. There was no doubt that males were first-class citizens in my extended family. Boys were destined to succeed in the business world; girls were reared to take their assigned place as wives and mothers in patriarchal society. My mother gave up her interest and considerable talent in art after she married. While she had no investment in being a housewife, she never worked outside the home and developed few interests apart from a vicarious enjoyment of some of her children's lives. My mother did not cook or clean house or sew. She hired helpers to take care of the house, including a nurse who had primary responsibility for the young children. My mother had very poor self esteem. My father, born and raised in Georgia, was a loud, passionate, creative man who was physically and emotionally cut off from his family of origin apart from infrequent visits to his father and stepmother and some connection to his older brothers and his stepbrothers. He was the fourth child in his family. The firstborn, a son, died in infancy; the second child, a daughter named Angel, died at age six when my father was an infant. His mother died in childbirth when he was six years old, leaving three young sons. Grandfather turned the children over to his mother and left for Mexico, where he worked as a land surveyor for a few years. Finally his mother insisted that he return to Savannah and find himself a new wife to take care of the boys. He did—and fathered five more children. Only years after my father's death and with the help of a therapist was I able to recognize that he was a depressed man whose dominance in any group he entered masked deep disappointment, loss, and grief. He had what I will later describe as false-self esteem. Both of my parents died in their fifties, just short of one year apart. Their untimely deaths of treatable illnesses could easily have been postponed.

At age four I entered kindergarten in a Roman Catholic convent school, where I remained until I graduated from high school. The religious women at school became my role models and authority figures. They were peaceful and prayerful and purposeful. They were also austere and mysterious and distant. They introduced me to God at an early age and consistently nurtured my interest in all things religious.

My engrossment in religious faith and issues of self esteem has increased over the years through my work as a teacher and counselor and through personal relationships. I have been particularly curious about the conflict between religious faith's claims about a God of love and believers' inability to love themselves. Many church leaders and churchgoers claim faith in a loving God who created and sustains the universe; belief in Jesus Christ, God-with-us, as the cosmic and personal redeemer; faith in the presence of the Holy Spirit in their lives; and the faith community, into which they have been received through baptism, as the nurturing, graced Body of Christ. They also hold the belief that human beings are made in the image of the holy God. Yet at the same time they see themselves as unworthy or unlovable people who do not deserve genuine, sustained happiness in life. One possible explanation for the paradox might be that conflicting images of God are at work in their psyches, canceling out the God of love.

Still other Christians claim that self esteem is incompatible with Christianity; that Christians are first and foremost unworthy sinners—"not okay" in the eyes of God—whose task is to humble themselves in submission before the throne of God. Sin is regarded as something to be punished, not a condition to be healed. In contrast, Rita Nakashima Brock calls sin "a sign of our brokenheartedness, of how damaged we are, not of how evil, willfully disobedient, and culpable we are."[1] A theology of submission and obedience which keeps God in "His" heaven and God's creatures in a constant state of repentance fosters an overemphasis on one's private relationship with an angry, exacting Deity. A God who does not want human beings to enjoy profound self-acceptance and self esteem is incompatible with a God of love, a God in love with the universe.

A study of the comments made on a self-esteem inventory questionnaire circulated among several groups of women and men (Appendix A) led me to the suspicion that what some people call "faith in God" or "faith in Jesus Christ" might be an escape from faith in self. Many people believe there is a close relationship between faith in God and the capacity to cope with life, as well as between their religious faith and their self esteem. Remarks such as these were written on the questionnaire: "God has pulled me through difficult times." "Self esteem follows when one gives all problems to the Lord to deal with." "You come to realize that even when times look hard, you can do all things through Christ." "God can make everything all right." One wonders what these individuals were thinking and feeling and doing when God took over their lives in this way.

What many women and men call faith in God is an escape from the need to establish a foundational belief in their own value and destiny and in their own innate capacity to respond to the challenges of life. Faith is too often used as a life preserver for people who are not sure they can really swim. Too many TV evangelists have connected religious faith with material success, health cures, and personal aggrandizement. Some students, too, talk about the connection between their religious faith and the experience of success or cures or special protection from illness or death. A rare few speak of discovering the incarnate Deity in themselves, of finding themselves empowered to respond to their own problems. Working with the results of the initial questionnaire shifted the focus of this inquiry from *faith and self esteem* to a study of *faith in self and self esteem*.

Faith in Self and Self Esteem

Religious faith does not contribute to self esteem unless it grows out of and along with faith in one's abilities, in one's intrinsic worth, in one's capacity for intimacy: out of and along with faith in oneself. Religious faith that is built on faith in oneself provides powerful motivation to join in the struggle to liberate anyone who is not free to enjoy such fullness of faith. This growing conviction overwhelmed me one privileged morning that stands out as a life-changing event.

A pilgrimage I took to Greece and the temples of the ancient goddesses set the stage for a grace-filled faith experience. Earlier during the week the four of us traveling together, half jesting, talked about the question each would ask the Oracle at Delphi, the ancient prophetess through whom the Deity was believed to have spoken words of wisdom. After winding our way up Mount Parnassus, through the miles and miles of olive trees covering the slopes, we drove into the town of Delphi with its streets of shops, restaurants, and hotels hugging the side of the mountain. Consulting our guidebooks, we read of Apollo's victory over the Earth Mother Ge or Gaia, whose shrine at Delphi was guarded by the dragon Python. The god Apollo killed Python and became lord of the sanctuary as Apollo Pythios. "This assumption of the sanctuary indicates that at this moment in the 9th c. B.C.

a male had supplanted the previously accepted female idol," the guidebook stated. The book went on to say that a woman still played a central role. Seated on a tri-pod above the cleft in the rock, she gave oracular utter-ances to those seeking her wisdom. Yet in the illustration that followed, the oracle is referred to as "it."[2] How easily the female pronoun disappears in patriarchal literature.

Early the following morning we arrived at the ancient ruins. Timbered slopes above us, we were already two thousand feet above the Gulf of Corinth when we started our tour, which led past the Roman market, through the gateway of the sacred precinct, and onto the path called the Sacred Way that leads to the temple of Apollo. The winding uphill route is lined with ruins of votive monu-ments to Apollo built by various Greek cities in gratitude for victory in battle. We strolled past the colonnaded buildings called treasuries, where offerings were stored. Next, the cone-shaped stone—the *omphalos*—believed to be the central point or navel of the world. My anticipa-tion grew until I spotted the scrubby rock pictured in the guidebook—the rock of the Sibyl where the Oracle re-sponded to the questions of those seeking her advice.

Standing on the Sacred Way beneath the rock of the Oracle in a place of overwhelming beauty and historical significance, I was transported to a time when rulers and prophets came to this very spot to seek her wisdom. No language adequately describes the event. It was a religious experience, a peak experience, a transcending experience. Yes, it was all of those—what happened within me was profound and life-changing, and I treasure it. I reflected on the self-esteem questions that have been of central im-portance to my personal and professional life over the last several years. At that moment my old friend self-doubt made no sense. Words could not express the sense of well-being that came over me. I was intensely aware that I am profoundly grateful for my husband and marriage; I was aware that I loved my friends (and I let many of their names and faces grace my imagination); that I loved my passion for justice; that I loved my life. I was simultaneously more aware and less aware of being an individual woman with a particular history and assets and liabilities. It was as if the fifty-five years of my life were all present and illuminated by a rush of faith in the goodness and holiness of life. I simply wanted to be where I was—in touch with the wisdom of woman, empowered by the gift of woman, there before the rock of the Sibyl and a stone's throw from the barely marked shrine of Earth Mother Ge, which I had not yet discovered.

Excited to be touched by the ancient past, thrilled to be on that pilgrimage, I was fully aware that I was experiencing a privileged moment. It was time outside time. I had a glimpse into a possible world in which women and men relate as equals, enjoying truly egalitarian relationships. Transcending a lifetime of both conscious and unconscious assumptions of women's second-class citizenship, I enjoyed a magnificent moment in which the wisdom, power, beauty, and bondedness of women were tangible. I felt a renewed confidence in my conviction that a major reason that religious faith does not help many women deepen their faith and respect in themselves is that most religious traditions have presented patriarchal or male-dominated theologies and ideologies.

A theology, or set of claims about Deity and the relationship between Deity and women and men, is always embedded in an ideology or understanding of the world and human beings' place in it. This book concerns both theology and ideology.

Institutional religions, echoing the patriarchal world in which they have thrived, have not only placed women beneath men on the hierarchy of being and value but also have failed to convince wombed and breasted women that they image life-giving Deity in profoundly symbolic ways. I had bought into that thoroughly patriarchal religion; I was lured out of it by the Holy One I call Goddess. I had a new understanding of the central feminist claim that the personal is political. That is, I saw through my personal struggle with self esteem and understood it as inextricably interwoven with the patriarchal world into which my parents were born, into which I was born, and in which the religion of my childhood and of the contemporary world has developed and continues to entrench itself. Aware of both the agony and the ecstasy of the experience, I cried in my heart as never before, "Oh, Goddess."

At that moment I had a new experience of the image of Goddess. While I have used the word *Goddess* to invoke and expand my understanding of the Deity, in Greece she became Earth Mother, Life Giver, the power and dignity and bondedness of women. "Pagan" and "idol" lost their negative power to divide me. I felt a remarkable connection between Goddess symbolism and a woman's self esteem.

When women image Deity in exclusively male terms, they relate to God (that is, male Deity) as "like the other but not like me." The symbols used of this Jewish and Christian male Deity or God are most often symbols of power and authority: Father, Lord, Ruler, and King. When women image Deity in female terms, however, they relate to Goddess as "like me." Symbols that speak of the Goddess are also powerful symbols but are more likely representative of nurturing and relational power and are perhaps more serene: Earth Mother, Life Giver, Comforter, Wisdom.

Evoking the Goddess can be enormously creative, challenging, and energizing. However, replacing male imagery of Deity with female images is not a long-term solution. Genuinely inclusive imagery is the only true solution. In the interim women need a transitional space in which they are able to claim the source of female beauty and power in Deity. The word *Goddess* refers to a female image; *God/dess* is an inclusive term including both masculine and feminine images of Deity. This book is about *faith*—faith in self and faith in God/dess that results in solid self esteem.

Dimensions of Self Esteem

Centrally, this is a book about self esteem. Self esteem is a universal issue that affects all people at some point in their lives, and most of us at many points in our lives. Two people I know claim that the only people interested in self esteem are those who do not have it. One person making that claim is a woman friend who is devastated by negative criticism. Another is a man with a strong tendency to dominate in social groups. Both have particularly strong confidence in their academic capacities and their leadership abilities. Both have blind spots that enable them to claim consistently high self esteem. The truth is that there is no such thing as consistently high self esteem, any more than there is consistent sunshine or joy or cheerfulness. Perhaps one of the problems lies in the large umbrella we open when we use the concept of self esteem.

Self esteem is a complex disposition that is related to at least six major experiences: (1) parental acceptance, (2) an ideology (an understanding of human life and one's place in it) that fosters self esteem, (3) satisfying relationships, (4) competence, (5) passion for life, and (6) self-acceptance.

The first of these is clearly the most crucial: namely, parental acceptance, love, and esteem of the infant and child. Unconditional acceptance is demonstrated through physical and emotional availability and the respect the parent shows for the child's full range of feelings. *Respect* is perhaps the key word in conveying the kind of acceptance I am describing. Acceptance that includes unqualified respect for the unique possibilities and budding personality of this child allows the child to develop its *true self*. In contrast, if parents set the agenda for who or what the child is to become, insisting on certain feelings or behaviors and forbidding others, the child develops a *false self* in order to defend herself or himself from the parents' judgment and thus assure their acceptance. Absolute acceptance of the child as the child discovers and expresses her- or himself results in what I call *good enough foundational self esteem.*[3] Without a healthy supply of it, the child suffers a deficiency that will play havoc with her or his self-evaluation. Low self esteem will continue unless the person, through some form of therapeutic process or an extraordinarily respectful relationship, or perhaps through the experience of belonging within a faith community, comes to an understanding of the deficit, and experiences radical acceptance and respect.

What will be discussed as foundational and secondary self esteem can be seen as parallel to what William James called once-born and twice-born believers. Persons with good enough foundational self esteem are the once-born who may go through life with a minimal amount of self-doubt or self-rejection. The twice-born need to be recreated, some of them many times over, through genuine mutual relationship. People who did not receive adequate positive parenting have a hard time being convinced of their intrinsic worth.

Second to parental acceptance, love, and respect, a child needs an ideology that fosters self esteem. While the parents give a child a sense of the world and the child's place in it, there is a universe beyond the home where the child must learn to live. The family worldview needs to be tested, developed, integrated, and owned or replaced as the child comes to her or his own understanding of human life and of society and how one fits in. Siblings and other relatives, friends, teachers, pastors—many people continue to contribute to one's self-understanding and values, which in turn shape self esteem. Social institutions of every kind also contribute to ideology. Media, advertising, theater, school, church, and the business world are constantly impinging upon the worldview of individuals with messages about who one is and should be, messages about both possibilities and limitations. An ideology can be read as a statement of one's values: It names what is good and true and valuable. For women, an ideology that fosters genuine self esteem must both recognize and celebrate their intrinsic worth as equal to that of men. The central thrust of the research that illuminates this book is an exploration of ideology and how it shaped the self esteem of a particular group of women.

The third component of self esteem is the capacity to develop and sustain mutually satisfying relationships, without which one remains unknown to self and others and disconnected. In their traditional roles as wives and mothers, women have long been recognized for their gifts and skill at developing and sustaining relationships. Today women seek new expressions of those profound relational abilities, within both marriage and single life, within family, within society, and, remarkably important, with one another in friendship and support groups.

The fourth component, competence, is understood as an individual's experience of achievement and success in meeting personal and social goals and expectations. The sense of competence begins as soon as the child tries to work with the things and ideas that fill its world: from building blocks to spoons and forks; from the alphabet and numbers to sand castles and bicycles; from examinations to a driver's license. For the woman rewriting an ideology, competence may mean preparing for career possibilities she never considered before, expressing her ideas in a male world, successfully coping with conflict in her life.

Passion for life, the fifth component of self esteem, is often related to a sense of vocation or purpose. One's passion for life takes different form through the various stages of an individual's life. Passion for life comes with discovering something worth knowing, worth doing, worth working toward. The opposite of passion for life is indifference, apathy, meaninglessness.

Finally comes self-acceptance, the sixth component of self esteem. Self-acceptance is used here in a specific way. It refers to the acknowledgment of one's physical and psychological givens as well as one's heritage: One's body, mind, emotion, spirit, and all that comes with being this particular person within this particular family in this particular time and place. Self-acceptance requires a realistic perception of those physical and psychological givens, a difficult task because so few people perceive themselves as others perceive them.

These multifaceted tasks and developmental issues set a lifelong agenda. For women it can be formidable. Throughout history (and for the most part even today) women have been educated into a patriarchal society where they learn to live as second-class citizens whose goal in life is to nurture husband, children, and others in need. Only in recent decades, and even then only in highly educated or politically active communities, have sufficient numbers of women awakened to and begun to expose the damaging effects of the domination/subordination soul of patriarchy.

One area where women might feel liberation from such structures is in seminaries. Women choosing seminary come with sufficient courage and conviction to aspire to become professional religious leaders in an area of the institutional church that has been and largely still is in the hands of a male clergy. The very presence of women seminarians reflects their sense of liberation and new possibility. Thus, it has not been surprising to hear a few female seminary students in their twenties argue that they did not grow up believing they are second-class citizens, and in fact presume that they can accomplish whatever they decide to accomplish—that gender is no issue. One reported that she only discovered the subordination of women firsthand when she began an internship in a local church. A second is convinced that her belief in women's ability, a strong message she consistently received from her mother, has motivated her to become so self-sufficient and accomplished that she has been unable to sustain an intimate relationship with a man. Any man, she is convinced, wants a more submissive, dependent wife than she would be able to become. This woman is caught in a love-hate relationship with her perception of herself as a strong, self-supporting woman who longs for an egalitarian relationship with a male life partner. One might wonder how long a local congregation would be at ease with her as a female pastor who did not plan to marry, were she to resign herself to staying single.

An increasing number of women recognize the need to create a new ideology, to rewrite their understanding of human life and of society and their place in it. Women need to see the world in a new way in order to come closer to their true selves and help others do the same. Revising an ideology can change many of the components that affect self esteem. Women who enjoy a good enough foundational self esteem, received through good enough parenting, may have but little work to do in revising patriarchal assumptions in their ideologies. Yet such revision might set them free for more passionate participation in the movement toward a just, egalitarian society. For women who did not begin life with adequate foundational self esteem, a revised ideology shaped within a caring relationship or support group or community can supply the needed vision to help them overcome their deficiency. An ideology can also supply the motivation women need to live fuller lives and to empower other women to do the same.

The Sample

Early in my work on this book, I recognized that while a pencil-and-paper questionnaire provided useful data for understanding how a person's belief system influenced her or his self esteem, what I really needed was indepth conversation with a sample of women. Inventory results lacked the concrete, interpersonal exploration and connection that has been the mark of feminist studies. Feminist theorists have moved from personal and interpersonal realities to the development of new paradigms for understanding and then returned to concrete reality to test those paradigms. Understanding the relationship between faith in self and self esteem required engagement with women who take faith issues seriously. The women who could best further this research would be those committed to discovering ways both to enhance their own self-understanding and to prepare themselves to care for the persons among whom they feel called to minister. The most obvious place to find such women was to seek them within the world in which I spend the major part of my time and energy.

Twenty-one women, ranging in age from twenty-four to sixty, were interviewed individually. All of the women were connected to an East Coast seminary. The majority were students, including a non-degree student in a lay resource course; three were staff persons or faculty. These women responded to a notice placed in the seminary newsletter asking for volunteers to participate in research on women's faith in self and self esteem. While a plurality of the women were United Methodist, the group represented a range of denominations—African Methodist Episcopal Zion, Episcopal, Metropolitan Community Church, Presbyterian, Southern Baptist, Unitarian Universalist, United Church of Christ—and also included a reform Jew. Seventeen women were Caucasian; four were African-American. The average age of the women was thirty-nine. Two women were in their twenties, ten in their thirties, seven in their forties, one in her fifties, and one, sixty. Eleven were married, five had never married, and five were divorced. Two of the women were lesbian.

No claim is made that this small sample represents the universe of women, nor will generalizations be drawn from the experience of twenty-one women. Far greater diversity in terms of cultural, social, and educational background would be necessary, and many more than twenty-one voices would have to be heard. Yet these women do form a small chorus and have powerful messages about the journey of a particular group of women living in a patriarchal society. The test of the conclusions drawn in this study will be whether the constructs provided by the conversations with a specific small chorus of women will echo in the lives of other women readers.

The Interview

In preparation for our interview, each woman received a memorandum containing questions or issues. While these open-ended questions could not possibly be covered in depth in a limited interview, they provided a focus for the sixty- to ninety-minute audiotaped session. The questions and issues were these:

A. Recall messages from parents, siblings, teachers, other significant adults, childhood and adolescent girlfriends and boyfriends; peer groups at various ages; close women and men friends; church, media, literature, health professionals; experience, study, reflection.

1. What significant messages come up for you about who you "should" be and/or who you are? At which stage of your journey were those messages most influential?

2. Are you conscious of conflicts you experienced between the ideology included in the messages you received and your capacity or desire to live it? How did you resolve the conflict?

B. When have you felt most alive, most engaged in life, most in touch with who you are and what you value?

C. What images of Deity and religious experience stand out for you: in your childhood, adolescence, young adult life, middle adult life? Are female images of Deity valuable to you?

The women were invited to begin the conversation wherever they wanted. In almost every case they began by articulating the messages they received from parent(s) about who they are and who they should be. By the end of the interviews, all had discussed what they have done with those messages. In every interview the women were asked to describe a time, at least one year in their past, when they felt particularly good about themselves and had notably high self esteem,[4] which was a variation of the question about a time in which they felt most alive, most engaged in life. The expectation was that the answer would reveal important aspects of each woman's ideology—that is, would illustrate values she held as particularly significant. As stories of the women will reveal, times when they felt particularly good about themselves often were instances in which they were able to enact some aspect of their evolving ideologies. In every interview images of God and the significance (or insignificance) of female images of Deity was discussed.

I had not anticipated the depth of empathy I would experience during my time with these women. I had taught most of them or known them through other work-related circumstances. The fact that we were talking as women about the struggle of women, and the poignant struggle of *this woman* who volunteered to reveal herself, set the stage for profound encounters. Often there were unexpected tears, as memories or present realities were brought forth. On the final day as I interviewed the last two women, I felt sadness that a particularly valuable part of my work was coming to an end. Yes, the power and dignity and bondedness of women can be overwhelming. I have deep gratitude for the women who joined me in this study.

The Flow of the Book

Chapter 1 offers an overview of the psychological processes through which people come to a sense of self and of their world and achieve or are deprived of *foundational self esteem*. The synthesis, based largely on the British psychoanalytic school known as object relations theory, has been written in language as nontechnical as possible. The writings of Alice Miller, a doctor of philosophy, psychoanalyst, writer, and painter, have been particularly informative in the perspective offered here on the journey toward self-understanding.

The second chapter explores images of God and how these affect a woman's self esteem. The work of psychiatrist and professor Ana-Maria Rizzuto has been especially helpful in coming to an understanding of the importance of God images, also called God representations, in the formation and evolution of faith life. In an effort to better understand the relationship between a woman's sense of self and language used of Deity, traditional Christian God language and God images are reviewed and expanded and more inclusive images suggested, and the God images of the women in the research group are explored.

Chapter 3 looks at the components of self esteem specifically from a woman's perspective. The term *good enough self esteem* is used to emphasize that self esteem is by nature in fluctuation because individuals are complex, creative, life-seeking, interdependent people, beautiful, and *incomplete* (a better word than flawed) and always changing. Stories from the lives of members of the research group highlight the significant connections among the components of self esteem and a woman's coming to faith in herself—especially her faith in herself as God image—and good enough self esteem.

Chapter 4 focuses still more closely on a group of women struggling with self esteem issues and largely surviving the struggle. On the downside, two major themes became evident in these women's lives. First is the drive for *unqualified approval*. In many cases this drive resulted in a self-defeating conviction that perfection is necessary for such approval. The drive for approval consequently expressed itself as a felt need to be perfect. Second, many of the women experienced *gender/sexual abuse*, a term that includes both physical and psychological sexual abuse, and any type of denigration of women. In its broad usage, gender/sexual abuse incorporates poor body image and body shame. On the upside, the women in the group repeatedly demonstrated courage, hope, and faith in new possibilities. The second half of chapter 4 includes more detailed stories of three of the women in the research group who illustrate the rediscovery of woman in a patriarchal society.

A final chapter recommends ways in which women suffering from low self esteem might work toward good enough true-self esteem. The overriding conviction of the three psychologists whose long-term work on self esteem was published by the American Psychological Association in a book titled *Self-Esteem: Paradoxes and Innovations in Clinical Theory and Practice* is used as a springboard. The difference between high self esteem and low self esteem, the authors suggest, comes down to the difference between choosing coping rather than avoidance when faced with conflicts that entail fear and anxiety.[5] Insights about the inadequate parenting a woman received as a child, or the second-class citizenship she has experienced in society, or the patriarchal theology that has misshaped her understanding of God, are not enough. Unless she determines to rewrite her ideology and live out of her new understanding of the world and her place in it, she will continue to perceive herself as not good enough. However, insight coupled with determination and the empowerment women so frequently receive through the support of other women can mean new life, a life graced by faith in self and self esteem.

1

Coming to
a Sense of Self

It is no exaggeration to say that from the very onset of
life the emergent human being is being catechized into a
cosmology—a sense of the way the universe runs and his
or her place in the scheme of things.

John McDargh[1]

It is no more an exaggeration to say that in its earliest
stages, the cosmology McDargh describes has everything to do with the individual's foundational self esteem. Many people think of "cosmology" as the work
of philosophers and astronomers—an obscure sort of
thing far removed from everyday life. A word like *ideology* might convey the same meaning as cosmology,
but, again, everyday people do not tend to articulate, in
any formal or comprehensive way, their ideology—
their conception of the world and of human life and of
themselves.

An ideology is a worldview that begins at the beginning, when parents consciously and unconsciously reflect
their beliefs and values to a child. Before the child has
discovered or named what it deems to be of value, except
perhaps the value an infant places on physical comfort, a
primitive understanding of the world is in the process of
being formed.

A developed ideology includes one's foundational beliefs about life, one's appropriated understanding of the rules and norms of society, and, critically important, one's view of oneself and one's place in the scheme of things. Many people spurt out particular claims or values relevant to religion or politics or sexual ethics when the conversation calls for it, but generally the overriding belief systems that rule human lives—considered thoughts and feelings about oneself, about one's responsibility for sisters and brothers and about the earth and air that human beings share—do not get much focused attention. And yet all people do in fact put their lives together out of an unwritten, perhaps unarticulated, and at times inconsistent and disorganized, philosophy of life. It takes motivation and effort to spell out what this cosmology or ideology looks like.

If the work has been going on since the onset of life, one wonders how it got started. And if a cosmology was underway from the very earliest years of life, one would speculate about how that primitive ideology relates to the ideology of adult life. Of particular significance to this study are the ideas a woman develops about herself, her true self and her false self, as well as ideas about others, the true other and the false other. Perhaps to find clues as to how ideas about both self and others take shape, an imaginary return to infancy and childhood would be of value.

A newborn infant has just left its utterly satisfying womb home and, through a life-threatening, totally disruptive process, has entered an alien new world. The baby seeks human contact. The baby seeks its mother: her warm body, her aroma, her breast, her face, her voice. The infant is compelled to connect with the most important person in the universe; the mother is eager for the same connection. Relational life has begun.

While the relationship between two individuals is indeed underway, at birth the infant is unable to distinguish itself from its mother or primary care-giver. Only gradually does she come to a primal understanding of her being as separate from that of her all-important provider, the center of her universe. Thousands of small interactions will take place over hundreds of days before the infant comes to an elementary sense of itself as separate from this powerful sustainer.

To simplify what is in fact a complex psychodynamic process, one might say that every exchange or encounter between mother and infant has both an objective and subjective side. The objective side is what takes place "out there" between mother and child. But the event that takes place on the outside is also experienced internally by both mother and child. The encounter may be perceived subjectively in markedly different ways. For example, a mother responds to her infant's need as she perceives it. Subjectively, her response is colored by whatever emotions she feels at the time she cuddles, nurses, cleans, or dresses her infant. She may be intensely present to her child; she may feel ill; she may be distracted or worried about someone or something else and have to muster the motivation to be responsive. The infant's subjective perception of her mother is also colored by the physical and emotional sensations she is experiencing on the inside. Her infant psyche is busily dealing with mother's gestures and words and tone of voice. Each of the interactions with mother is remembered as mostly rewarding or mostly frustrating; at times totally rewarding or totally frustrating. Some part of the infant takes in some part of mother. The infant may have a felt need to be stroked and cuddled; the mother's warm, tender response is tucked away in the infant's memory bank: content, lovable me and comforting, tender mother. On another occasion the hungry infant is not satisfied by mother's breast or bottle and cries itself into a desperate rage: hungry, lonely me and cruel, rejecting mother.

Since the infant is so critically dependent on the good mother for survival, she protects herself from these negative memories by splitting them off from the good memories and repressing them or erasing them from consciousness.[2] Splitting the infant's internal world into fragmented memories is a protective strategy that the infant unconsciously uses for survival. While both the infant's unmet need and the mother's negative response are repressed together, the infant carries a vague, unconscious memory that she—the infant—is bad, for it is safer to consider oneself bad than to reject one's life source. Rejection of mother or father is unthinkable because it would amount to rejecting the only world one knows. These repressed experiences then result in the infant's unconscious rejection of herself: bad me. (Battered children's attempts to deny that their parents are abusive is a good indication of the splitting process. They erase the abuse from memory and cling to what is left of their split, idealized parent—better than no parent at all.) Consciously, the infant continues to seek satisfaction from her "ideal" mother, that is, the mother she has not repressed, and continues to seek her mother's face and breast and hands.

Psychologists have used the word *mirroring* to describe the mother-child interaction in which the mother, through eye contact and absorbed presence to the infant, gives her a sense of being seen, recognized, and understood. The baby seeks the mother's face in order to know who the baby is. It is as if the baby is saying to the mother, "Tell me who I am." The mother mirrors back to the baby, "You are my precious child." Each is also saying to the other, "You are centrally important to me." When the mother looks at the baby she holds—whether she cherishes or resents the responsibility she carries for this child—the expression on her face is a reflection of what she sees in her arms.[3] Whatever the mother is feeling inside is projected onto the child, and whatever the child sees on its mother's face is internalized. In other words, a delighted mother visibly reflects her delight in her presence to the baby; a brokenhearted, despairing mother reflects pain and desperation. The child internalizes either delight or pain and desperation.

Both mother and infant find themselves mirrored in

the face of the other. If the mother is overanxious or is feeling particularly needy herself, she will be unable to bracket her own wants or concerns or pain and be fully open and present to the child. She will be unable to allow the child to freely emerge through the expression of both positive and negative feelings. She will be unable to learn from her infant what this child is experiencing, and unable to learn more about her own emotional life in the process. What she mirrors back to the child is some expression of her needs or her agenda, not an understanding of the child's emerging self-discovery and mother-discovery. The process is contaminated by mother's emotions to the extent that the child is not allowed to find herself in mother's face. Instead of a transparent, child-focused face, the child finds a cluttered, self-absorbed face.

Enormous power is in the hands of parents; in the earliest months in the hands of the primary nurturer, "our earliest relationships can steal our true selves or mirror them back to us."[4] Respectful affirmation of the child in its vulnerable infancy is all-important to the child's ability to be its true self and experience foundational self esteem. Otherwise the child senses that it must comply to mother or father's blatant or subtle demands and pursue a false self. Through mirroring an ideology is formed, a worldview that informs the child as to what is expected of it and gives the child a sense of her or his place in mother's and father's lives and in the world.

For example, the child may learn over the first few years of life that she or he is responsible for mother's happiness, that only happy feelings are truly acceptable, that if mother is sad or depressed, the child has failed. Or the child may learn that life is a great adventure, that all feelings can be freely expressed, with mother there as witness, companion, and intimate partner in the ongoing discovery.

Alice Miller, who writes passionately and persuasively about the needs of the child, warns that if the mother mirrors only her own expectations, the child remains without a mirror and seeks in vain for the rest of her life for someone who can make up for what mother failed to do.[5] Yet because the messages the child hears from mother and then father are all-important to the understanding of her or his place in the parents' lives, the child who does not receive adequate mirroring learns to adapt to the parents' wants and needs.

In other words, if a child is told that only babies cry or that anger is unacceptable or that she cannot say she hates a parent, or simply that mother considers her to be a burden, then the sadness that triggers the tears, the intense anger, and verbal expressions of hate become split off and repressed. The child fights back tears and wears a smile, says "I love you" when she or he means "I am so angry at you that right now I hate you." The child develops what theorists call a *false self*, an adapted self who lives according to other people's expectations. The false self accommodates to parental needs, losing touch with authentic wants and needs, and is rewarded for making the adaptation. Miller calls the false self an "as-if personality" that keeps the *true self* in a state of noncommunication.[6]

The true self, elusive because it is always in the process of becoming, begins to emerge with the authentic expression of feelings, sensations, and needs, which later become the authentic expression of ideas and emotions. The primitive capacity to feel one's needs and communicate them is the earliest sense of self, one's "experience of aliveness."[7] When the expressed need is accepted, the true self begins to unfold. When the expressed need is rejected, the true self is violated. The damaged true self is then protected and hidden by the false self with its defensive feelings and needs.

Within the first few years of life, an ideology or cosmology takes shape in the child's psyche that will result in the child feeling free to develop creatively her or his capacities, gifts, and interests, *or* sensing an obligation to adapt to the needs and desires of its primary caretakers. More likely, the child will both be "catechized" into the parents' worldview and the parents' hopes for the child's place in that world and at the same time find room in that cosmology for her or his unique contribution to the scheme of things.

None of us received perfect parenting. None of us gives perfect parenting. The phrase *good enough mothering* (or *good enough parenting*) is used to indicate that the most any child will receive is a favorable balance of responsive, respectful presence over frustrating, rejecting parental behavior. However, the rejecting behavior is not the more injurious aspect of the child's experience. Rather, the harm is done when the child is forced to repress her or his anger. "The greatest cruelty that can be inflicted on children is to refuse to let them express their anger and suffering except at the risk of losing their parents' love and affection." Miller goes on to say that such lack of freedom leads to suicide and drug addiction.[8]

On the other hand, when the child is shown genuine respect, which includes respect for and an invitation to express all of her feelings, she has learned something that is transferable to all other relationships. Miller believes that this respect is a profoundly educational, formational experience: "If a mother respects both herself and her child from [the] very first day onward, she will never need to teach [her child] respect for others."[9]

Miller's haunting words resound again and again a plea to parents to respect the child.

> The child has a primary need to be regarded and respected as the person he really is at any given time, and as the center—the central actor—in his own activity . . . we are speaking here of a need that is narcissistic, but nevertheless legitimate, and whose fulfillment is essential for the development of a healthy self-esteem. . . . Parents who did not experience this climate [atmosphere of respect and tolerance for feelings] as children are themselves narcissistically deprived; throughout their lives they are looking for what their own parents could not give them at the correct time— the presence of a person who is completely aware of them and takes them seriously, who admires and follows them.[10]

Parents can unconsciously use their children to try to make up for what was lacking in their own childhood. When a parent attempts to reverse roles with a child, that is, expects the child to do for the parent what her or his own parents did not do, the child is burdened with responsibility that can distort her or his whole life. The parent tries to make up for her or his own deprivation and in so doing deprives the child, who resorts to a false self rather than no self at all. The child's legitimate and appropriate need to be accepted as she really is gets eclipsed by the parent's legitimate but inappropriate need for the child to make up for what the parent missed as a child: "the presence of a person who is completely aware of them and takes them seriously, who admires and follows them." The often subtle message is "need me," "cling to me," "make me happy." The parent, operating out of a false self, is expecting the wrong things from the child, encouraging in the role reversal that the child too become a false self. Since many people operate out of a largely false self, they look for a reflection of their false selves in the eyes of the other, who in turn becomes a false other—the person one needs in order to maintain a false self.

The child who is pressured into being a submissive, obedient, polite, and cheerful daughter will look for affirmation from her instructors: "I've done it. Now tell me I am the perfect little girl you want me to be." The child who grew up accommodating will expect the same from the next generation. And so the process repeats itself generation to generation, unless or until the adult is able to rework her or his early relationships through a therapeutic process, or through a remarkably healthy adult relationship, or perhaps through the support of an empathic, affirming group.

One way, then, of managing long-repressed needs is to attempt to have them met through one's children. Another unconscious device is to project the repressed memories of negative interactions with parents onto other significant people in the adult's life. For example, the child who was never allowed to express hostility toward a parent will have difficulty in recognizing and expressing hostility as an adult. The adult, unaware of long-repressed anger, may have a distorted perception of a spouse as the hostile one, and herself or himself as the rejected, bad, guilty person. In other words, the anger is projected onto a convenient target. Neither person will understand why seemingly insignificant interactions between them escalate into full-scale conflicts. A desire for the ideal parent will also be projected, and the person seeking such total responsiveness from a partner will undoubtedly be disappointed. Making up for the deprivation of childhood by turning a spouse into a parent simply does not work. The truth is that there is no way to make up for a lack of attention and love, legitimate needs that were not adequately met in childhood. However, unless the damage was severe enough to destroy the ability to trust and hope, people can come to understand their journeys—deprivations and disappointments included—and live with more realistic expectations within their relationships to children and adults.

In the past, I sometimes reacted negatively to persons saying things such as, "There's a part of me that wants to do this; another part wants to do that." It made more sense to see people as wholes and not parts and to use language such as "mixed feelings" to describe such conscious ambivalence. The theory briefly outlined here supports the reality that indeed human beings are many parts and yet one. The word *part* aptly describes a conflicted aspect of the inner life as people struggle to understand, to make decisions, and to act on their decisions. Those parts came to birth during the very early months and years when children first learned to relate to others and to begin to know themselves as separate individuals *essentially* connected to other separate individuals, all of them complex, their memory banks filled with both positive and negative experiences of their parents and themselves. The difficulty in understanding some of one's own reactions lies in the fact that many early frustrating, even devastating interactions have been erased from conscious memory, and as an adult, one is left with no clear idea as to how much one's present is shaped by these repressed memories.

This discussion has focused primarily on the power of the primary care-giver in the life of the newborn and child. Society's belief that the mother must be the primary care-giver has been challenged by feminists, notably by psychologist Nancy Chodorow. Chodorow has written persuasively that apart from the significant bodily functions of the mother in gestation, childbirth, and lactation, the father can be equally involved in the parenting process. Many couples have demonstrated that the parenting of infants and children can indeed be an equally shared responsibility, with both father and mother participating in all aspects of family life. Studies indicate, however, that in dual-career marriages in which parents aim toward shared parenting and housekeeping, women generally carry most of the responsibility for the home. Froma Walsh reports that wives who work outside the home continue to carry 80 percent of the household and child-care responsibilities, including an overall coordinating of family life.[11] Another study concludes that full-time housewives average 8.1 hours a day in household work. Women employed outside the home average 4.8 hours. Husbands, however, spend 1.6 hours a day in household work whether their wives work outside the home or not.[12]

In addition to fostering egalitarian relationships and overcoming gender restrictions, Chodorow underscores another important benefit to be gained when fathers develop intimate relationships with infants through shared child care. When mothers alone are the primary nurturers, male children discover their identity through an experience of being different from their mothers and needing to separate from them in order to come to a sense of themselves as male. Were fathers equally involved in the parenting, their sons would enjoy the same kind of intimacy available to girls who discover themselves to be the same as mother, not in need of an "over against" experience to appropriate their gender identity.[13]

In addition to strong shaping by mothers and fathers, children are catechized by numerous other people in their expanding worlds: siblings, grandparents, other relatives, neighbors, teachers, pastors, friends, and parents of those friends. Explicitly or implicitly, most of these people, through what they do and say and how they live, transmit messages about the universe and the child's place in it. The messages continue throughout life. The focus of this study is on the memories that can be called up to consciousness for reworking. One hopes this process will allow some of the repressed memories of any person seeking to rewrite an ideology to surface and be reworked.

To sum up, the self is a concept that defines what is most personal and unique about an individual. People do not *have* a false self nor a true self that they can take out and show one another; they *are* their selves, and those selves are always in process, always changing, each unique. The self includes the body, mind, and spirit; abilities and limitations; and repressed and remembered experiences both positive and negative: bodily experience, relational experience, cultural experience, religious experience. People are themselves, some combination of true self—that is, the unique aliveness experienced at the deepest level of the human psyche, hinting at the realistic possibilities of who they might become—and false self, either an idealized image others have held up to them as to who they ought to be or a negative image of the failure others have predicted they will become. Their task is to find a favorable ratio of true self over false self so that they can enjoy good enough self esteem and through mutual relations help others do the same.

The Study

To facilitate the process by women in this study of coming to a better sense of the *false selves* they had constructed over their lives, as well as the *true selves* that continue to emerge, each woman was asked to recall some of the messages from her childhood. All of the women were able to highlight pivotal themes, and in the process each could see the difference between the aspects of an ideology that came from significant others and from society and the ideology she has intentionally been rewriting as an adult.

Many of the stories of these women's lives illustrate the revising of an ideology. Some of the women have transformed their lives; others continue the struggle. Here are three of these women. Glenda is living what she would call a resurrected life. Celine is along the road in her journey. Kit is setting out on her new path.

Glenda is a white, thirty-nine-year-old nurse practitioner working with children who have cancer. She grew up in an unhappy home with an alcoholic father who was both verbally and physically abusive and a mother she perceived to be weak, helpless, and hopeless. From her father Glenda picked up the message that she was simply not good enough. Nothing satisfied him, but she was expected to keep trying to win his approval. From her mother she learned that a woman is dependent upon a man and has no power to lead a life apart from him. A woman's decision as to who that man will be is irreversible: Once she marries she has made the bed she must stay in. In other words, she must look to a man for her fulfillment, but she will inevitably be disappointed in her relationship.[14]

Glenda set herself the task of converting her father and thereby saving her powerless mother as well. "If I was good enough, something would motivate him to stop drinking. I was supposed to be good . . . like *I* was making him drink." Glenda was fiercely faithful to her mission well into adulthood. Her father left her mother for another woman, but his drinking only escalated.

Exceptionally successful at work, Glenda says she was a dismal failure in developing a relationship with a man and found herself deeply depressed. A coworker suggested a possibility Glenda had not seriously considered by telling her that people go to therapists to work through depressions. By the end of her ninety-two hours of work with a woman therapist, Glenda had not only recognized the impossible responsibility she had taken for her father's life, she had also developed a healthy intimate relationship with the man she later married. Since then Glenda has become the mother of a daughter, now two years old.

A turning point came in her therapy when she recognized that her "hope was hopeless," that is, Glenda wanted for her father what he did not choose for himself. In her language, she decided to give up on him—but actually she gave up on her need to save him. She put clear boundaries within their relationship, insisting that if he had been drinking when she arrived to visit him, she would leave. Often she left. Sometimes she stayed to visit with her sober father.

Glenda is proud of her journey from being a depressed woman with a pervasive sense of failure to being a fulfilled wife and mother and nurse, a strong woman enjoying good enough self esteem. She says with deep satisfaction, "I can be happy. I am very happy with my husband and my child, and I would be very unhappy if I did not have them—but I could manage."

It is not hard to imagine what might have happened if Glenda's father had become a recovering alcoholic and her mother had established herself in a more satisfying life. Glenda surely would have felt good about herself. The question is whether her self esteem would have endured if father or mother had regressed to alcoholism or hopelessness. In other words, if Glenda's self esteem was dependent upon her parents' recovery, she was motivated by false-self demands. The distinction between true-self esteem and false-self esteem, developed in the next chapter, rests on whether the events triggering the self esteem are based on an owned, realistic ideology or the impossible expectations of an unreasonable ideology.

While Glenda has successfully abandoned the false

self that required her to meet unrealistic goals, Celine is in the midst of effecting the changes she is still writing into her revised ideology.

Celine, fifty-two, African-American, is a strong introvert who grew up with a clear sense of what her parents wanted and expected from her. At the core of the family value system was success, and for school-age children, success was measured and demonstrated through an excellent academic and extracurricular record. Also high on the list were honesty, obedience, and conformity. Celine consistently rose to the occasion. Her accomplishments included excellent grades, leadership roles in school organizations, scouting, piano, voice, and acting as well as exemplary conduct. When she graduated from junior high school she was valedictorian, and she finished high school third in a class of 360.

> In high school I was in Honor Society, the recipient of Quill and Scroll, a winner in oratorical contests. . . . I taught Sunday school and got a certificate. Whenever I got a certificate I felt very good.

In adult life Celine continued her successful achievements. Starting out as a clerk-typist for a governmental agency, she moved up through the ranks—but only as far as an African-American was likely to go at that time. She watched her Caucasian trainees become her supervisors. In spite of her achievements, Celine knew something was missing.

> At some point it became obvious to me that I could be successful in doing all that, but I wasn't really successful at life itself. . . . I think I was really just afraid of making relationships.

What she had not developed was the ability to enter into emotionally intimate relationships. In addition to the fact that the family did not discuss personal problems or fears, both of Celine's parents died before she was twenty years old. She was beginning to get emotionally close to them when she lost them. She never felt emotionally close to either her brother or sister.

Celine married a man with whom she was unable to reveal herself. As she put it, she chose the wrong person. She perceived that her husband was jealous of the time she wanted to give to her interests in music, reading, and singing in choir. There was little communication or understanding between them, and Celine made a decision that broke with family ideology: she left her marriage of seven years. The family did not consider divorce an option. In fear that she would not be accepted, she then cut herself off from her extended family. Celine had neither faith in herself nor the support of a community that would allow her to revise her ideology and accept what she had done.

Reconnecting with a male high school friend when they were in their forties set the stage for what Celine calls a spiritual conversion. The two of them read scripture and prayed together. Celine became powerfully aware of God's presence in her life, which she said brought an indescribable feeling of "joy, elation, and peace." She determined to reestablish relationships with relatives and friends. However, while Celine is aware of notable progress in her engagement with others, she still struggles with a fear of intimacy, that is, a fear of revealing herself and a reluctance to trust that a relationship will endure. Bridging the gap between a revised ideology and learned behavior is requiring years of hard work on Celine's part.

A third example is Kit, a twenty-five-year-old white woman. Kit's adolescence was shattered by family disruption and complicated by ideological shifts within her family of origin. Her task of both revising her ideology and implementing it is only beginning.

Kit explained that she was successfully indoctrinated into wanting to be very much "a little girl"; dolls and playing house were an important part of her childhood. The catastrophic event that threw her life into chaos was her parents' unexpected divorce at her father's initiative when she was twelve, after which her mother "went through a feminist consciousness-raising."

"I being the only daughter," Kit said, "she took me with her on that [journey]." Kit's sense of responsibility for her mother's happiness was already well in place. "The hardest thing about the divorce," Kit explained, "was that she was so unhappy." A basic message Kit heard from her mother was that she had best not conform to society's expectations because "being female is not that good." It's more important, her mother would say, "to go out and prove yourself in a male world." Thus, after twenty years of being housewife and mother, her mother developed a business profession.

Meanwhile, Kit knew that her brothers were not getting along with her mother and sensed that her role was to be the family peacemaker. Perhaps another reason Kit took on the role of peacemaker was that her mother turned her face outward while the family was filled with loss and grief. Kit was aware of a vacuum in the family. Playing the role of diplomat brought the approval of the whole family. She "tried to get everyone comfortable": her two older brothers, her mother, her father, and eventually her father's new wife. Kit's care-giving included reversing roles with her mother and becoming mother's confidant and counselor. "I was more of a support for her than she for me." Her mother denigrated the traditional role a woman plays in both family and the world outside the home, saying that nurturing is less valuable than establishing oneself in the male world. At the same time she ironically turned to Kit, both expecting and rewarding nurture and female companionship as she struggled through her divorce. It was as if she were saying, "I'm asking you to be the kind of young woman that I do not find valuable."

Confused about her identity, Kit tried all the harder to be perfect in her schoolwork, her music, her role as family care-giver. She cannot remember a time when she was not a perfectionist: "People would tell me good things and I would say that they don't really know me." (Kit's need to please showed up repeatedly during the interview. Over and over she asked if she were performing according to expectations: "I don't know if that helps." "Am I going in the right direction?" "Should I go on?" Her concluding words were "I'm feeling badly that maybe you didn't get to ask some questions you wanted to ask.")

Kit's current struggle is that of trying to let go of her impossible expectations and believe that she is an imperfect but very lovable woman. She is yet to be truly convinced that love is not won and maintained through perfection. After ending a number of significant relationships with men, she has decided to work on herself in therapy before she suffers through another relationship in which she denies that she is a good enough partner and lives in fear that the person who cares for her will disappear.

Glenda, Celine, and Kit are women at different stages in the necessary process of revising their ideologies in order to believe in their intrinsic value and live more realistic and satisfying relational lives. Developing an adequate ideology, especially for women of faith, invariably includes a reappropriation and, for most of the women in this study, a transformation of one's images and understanding of Deity. The following chapter is a consideration of the role that images of God play in a woman's ideology and therefore in her self esteem.

2

God Images
and the
Self Esteem of Women

Across this "night of the fathers" now streaks a comet—
the outbreaking of the feminine in the emergence of
women's spirituality in our era. What is happening
among many women of many cultures is preparing the
ground for a new Genesis, a new God myth: the return
to God the Mother; the return to earth and embodiment;
the revaluation of personal experience . . . the return to
relation and connection.

Madonna Kolbenschlag[1]

Who introduced you to God? That question proved to
be a provocative one for senior high school students in a
Roman Catholic school. Disciplined to give word-perfect
answers to the God-questions in the Baltimore Catechism
of the Roman Catholic Church, they were caught off
guard when asked to try to retrieve memories of either a
conversation about God or a time when they became
aware of a "supreme being." Some drew blanks. Others
recalled classroom or church experiences where they
were "given the truth." Very few remembered becoming
intrigued by ultimate questions or concerns. One wonders what would happen if parents and teachers waited
for children to ask God-questions before giving God-
answers. A friend who taught religion teachers at the

catechetical institute in Nijmegen, the Netherlands, pleaded with his students who taught first grade to refrain from mentioning God until the children did. If the children did not raise the question before Christmas, my friend Frans conceded, the teacher could initiate the conversation by telling the Nativity story. "But what will we teach?" the religion teachers asked anxiously. Frans suggested that the teachers help the children explore their world, beginning with learning one another's names, appropriating the classroom, rearranging desks and other furnishings. Next, the class might be taken on a "field trip" throughout the school, including a visit to the principal's office. Once the children "owned" their immediate surroundings, teachers were encouraged to explore with them in fantasy the service institutions throughout the city. "Imagine that it is midnight. Where are lights still burning? Why are these people not in bed?" Expand the children's imaginations, root them in their community, broaden their world, and the God-question will surely come into the classroom.

While the God-question may not emerge until the child first enjoys the marvelous gift of wonder, God images have been in the process of formation long before the question is raised. Both the early formation of God images and the answers the child is given by parents, siblings, or religious educators are profoundly related to faith in self and self esteem.

The Psychological Formation of God Images

In a ground-breaking work on the formation of God images, *The Birth of the Living God*, Ana-Maria Rizzuto[2] explains how early interaction with parents, which results in both positive and negative memories or representations of oneself and one's parents, are the primal stuff that gets worked into God representations or God *imagos*. These images may or may not be compatible with later ideas about God introduced by parents, religious educators, or theologians and artists who try to express in religious symbols and imagery their conceptions of the sacred in human life.

In the language of the object relations school of thought out of which Rizzuto works, children rely on memories (or internalized objects)—namely, internalized aspects of their parents and themselves—to help them function in their world. A memory of mother or father, stored along with memories of having been loved by her parent, sustains the child during the absence of the parent. Sometimes a concrete object such as a blanket, a stuffed animal, or a piece of clothing is used as what is called a *transitional object*. The object helps the child bridge the gap between inner perceptions and memories and outer reality, as well as between the private parent-child world and the world peopled by other family members and even strangers. The clutched blanket or toy is truly a security-evoking blanket or toy. Strengthened by memories of her caretakers and armed with a special symbol of her powerful providers, the child moves about in what is called *transitional space*. Transitional space refers to the time of psychological progression from a private inner world of infancy to an expanding outer world of childhood. Rizzuto says that children around the age of two or three populate their transitional space with an abundance of fascinating creatures—God among them.[3]

If parents, the child's first religious educators, wait for the child to raise ultimate questions before using God language, they will probably wait until the three-year-old begins to ask ceaseless questions of causality: Where do animals come from? Who made the sky? Where did the sun come from? How are babies made? God, the supreme being responsible for such wonders, is naturally imaged by the child as the most powerful person(s) she knows, that is, as somewhat like the parent(s) but larger and greater. Many memories and experiences go into early God images: characteristics of the parents and of siblings and other relatives, the good experienced in ourselves and others, the religious and intellectual culture of the home, and circumstances present in the child's life.[4]

Illustrating how particular incidents can influence a God representation, Rizzuto says,

> A striking example could be an impressive summer storm after the child has had his first conversation with his mother about God. The child may experience the storm as God's personal show of frightening power or anger. In one of the cases studied, the opposite experience, of being under God's protection, was triggered by the equally irrelevant circumstance of finding a penny in the street after the child had asked God to provide for him.[5]

Rizzuto helps answer a question raised in the introduction of this book, that is, why faith in a loving God can fail to result in positive self esteem. She distinguishes between God representations or internalized *imagos* and the rational ideas about God (theology and dogma). A third level of experience contributes to one's God conception, namely, the God convictions one holds as the result of religious experience. One might speculate as to how these three levels of God imagery work themselves out in the life of a child.

For example, one could assume that a child's early experience of her angry, verbally abusive father resulted in a representation of authority as exacting, threatening, and punishing. The child's felt reactions to authority—that is, to her father—take the form of an unconscious representation of ultimate Authority. To this child, father is ultimate authority. The child internalizes, along with bad, frightening father, a negative self-representation: bad me, worthy of punishment. Her negative father/authority representation is in place and will become her unconscious representation of God/authority.

While her fear of authority is well established, the child meets with other ideas about ultimate Authority. At the dinner table, in Sunday school, and through Bible stories read to her at night, she is taught that God is a loving, caring "person" or being who is all-knowing and all-powerful. Some of these words about God might reinforce her unconscious God image: God is all-knowing and all-powerful—from God there is no escape. Others are in contrast to the punishing God representation: God is loving and caring. Then the child is awakened to the presence of God through an experience of nature. Her cat gives birth to kittens. Day after day, the child's mother spends hours with her daughter. They read a book about cats; they watch their beloved cat nurse her newborn kittens. With mother's gentle tutoring, the little girl learns to hold very tenderly her favorite kitten. The child marvels at the wonder of life and at her strong connection to these tiny, fragile balls of fur with sticky eyes opening to make contact with her own. Caught up in mystery, the child has a transcending experience of a holy presence.

However, she continues to live with fear in her heart that she will "cause" her father to lose his temper, that she will fail in her attempts to please him. And she continues to leaf through her book of Bible stories, asking questions about the loving God who knows all things. Every night she prays that God will watch over the family and especially the kittens.

One might speculate as to who God is to this young girl. A person with such conflicting experiences could expound a very positive concept of God that is in sharp contrast to an unconscious, exacting, punishing God representation that grew out of early parental interaction. She may express faith in a loving, caring, intimate God, but undermine her faith in self by keeping alive a cruel, demanding God representation. The negative God representation has both a longer history and a stronger emotional hold on the child's psyche; loving, caring, intimate God will not prevail until the negative God representation has been recognized, confronted, and replaced. If a negative God representation is compounded by negative ideas about a judging God, so much greater is the person's self-contempt and self-rejection.

One might wonder whether a reverse situation could not also occur. A child begins life with a very positive image or representation of authority that is in conflict with negative ideas about God learned through church or school. Undoubtedly this could be the case. However, with predominantly positive authority images, a child will develop good enough self-images and God images to withstand any poisonous concept of God presented by authority figures in the child's life. Perhaps the struggle will include confusion and the need for ongoing reinforcement of the respectful relationship that resulted in a positive God representation in infancy. Perhaps the child will find negative God simply incredible—she might later call herself atheist or agnostic in reaction to such a deity.

The fantasy of a child struggling with conflicted ideas and experiences of authority finds an echo in the lived experience of one of the women in the research group. In Jessica's home, dominated by her father, perfection was the key to acceptance. She knew she should be perfect and should do everything right the first time. Her attempts to be perfect, however, were complicated by the fact that her father was unpredictable and inconsistent, and his dissatisfaction frequently resulted in physical violence. She and her brothers went to great pains to second-guess what perfection meant from day to day, over and over again failing to live up to her father's standards of the hour.

> I'd get furious when he'd come home and we would shudder, not knowing what was going to happen when he walked through the door and whether we'd been perfect enough or not. Sometimes when he would come home, everything—the peace and tranquility of the house—would just be totally disrupted and we would find ourselves being beaten for not having washed a cup or for not having said "hello" soon enough.

Regardless of the gender of the parent or child, physically or psychologically violent parenting will result in a child's formation of a cruel and exacting representation of authority and therefore of God. The victim of such abuse will need some form of re-parenting; that is, someone will need to help the child or adult through a new experience of authority. Someone will need to offer nurturing, accepting, encouraging support. Through re-parenting, the adult can come to a realistic understanding of who she is and who she might become. In cases of severe deprivation or overt abuse, re-parenting may require a long-term therapeutic relationship. Only after an experience of dependable care and respect will the deprived person be able to believe positive God words. For women open to the possibility, female God words can enhance the process of coming to woman-acceptance and self-respect.

While in most cases church people find it difficult to shift from well-established male images of God to more inclusive images, sometimes the experience is the opposite. A student pastor reported such an experience after years of taking her children to carefully chosen congregations in which she found awareness of both racial and gender justice. They worshiped in churches which used inclusive language first in referring to humankind and then, in step with new consciousness, in reference to the Deity. Midway through seminary she began an internship in a suburban church. She and her son worshiped at her new church for the first time. She was concerned about her son's reactions during the service of worship, which was far more conservative than that to which the family had become accustomed. On the way home he asked, "Mom, why do the people in that church think God is a man?" This fortunate child had already grown accustomed to a wide range of images of God. It was upsetting for him to worship with people whose vision was much narrower than his own. He was eager for them to become educated.

Self esteem is related to all three levels of God imagery: unconscious God representations formed through the child's interaction with her parents, ideas about God learned through socialization, and the experience of God in one's life. While all three levels or layers of God knowledge are potent, the unconscious representations of God and self may have the strongest impact on good enough self esteem. Early images or representations of parents and self are invariably distorted. These images shape early God representations. When negative images predominate, they can so reduce one's ability to believe in self that anything one learns about God in later life seems unbelievable. However, faulty representations can be consciously reshaped in adult life through relationships in which a person is realistically perceived and treated with respect. Through positive relationship, a person can be helped to move away from the poor representation of self which led to the pursuit of false self and toward a realistic representation of self that encourages the expression of the true self. Parallel to that accomplishment, one is able to leave behind a negative God representation which results in the creation of a *false God* and move toward a positive God representation which allows one to discover the *true Deity*.

This consideration of the psychological processes that initiate the formation of God imagery is followed by a review of cultural images of God and religion that mold additional layers of a child's God concept.

Patriarchy and Theological/Ecclesial Images of God

God imagery is extremely complex. Rizzuto illuminates the process whereby children begin life with an assortment of early representations of parent and God. These images or *imagos* remain hidden beneath both conscious and sleeping ideas about God handed on through the family, the Bible, church, and school. Ideas about God are made immediate through lived experience that most intensely teaches people about God (religious experience or revelation). In addition, through all the layers are the effects of a patriarchal mind-set that have dramatically influenced every aspect of human life, including God imagery.

The only society that anyone who was raised in Western civilization has ever known is a patriarchal society.

The word *patriarchy* applies to any society in which the father is the supreme or final authority and in which wives and children are legally dependent upon him. In patriarchal societies, descent and inheritance are reckoned in the male line. One might take issue with the claim that the only society known to Western people is a patriarchal one; one could point out specific cases and even whole subcultures in which the mother is effectively the head of the family. However, the fact of the man's financial responsibility for his family, as well as that of descent and inheritance through the male line, would apply even in cases in which a matriarch rather than patriarch actually dominates an individual or extended family. In addition, the family or subculture ruled by females is itself immersed in a larger patriarchal society in which the majority of elected and appointed leaders are men and in which men are more highly valued than women. In other words, patriarchy is so pervasive that it could be used as a synonym for the broadest use of the word *society*.

At the heart of patriarchy, as the definition suggests, is the hierarchical position of sovereign males over dependent females. When patriarchal value judgments are projected onto a supreme being, Deity is automatically imaged in male terms.

The central point to be made here is that gender assumptions are pervasive in patriarchal societies. Gender assumptions pervade the parent-child relationship. Cultural attitudes toward the role of women in society have an impact on the way parents raise both their sons and their daughters. Gender matters slant religious beliefs: an exclusively male God perpetuates a male-dominated hierarchy. Gender distortions may even contaminate the positive lived experiences that teach people most intensely and persuasively about God. A woman convinced of her second-class citizenship can easily find herself in worship seeking crumbs from the master's table (see Mark 7:28). As long as one gender is seen as subordinate and the other dominant, the gender assumed to be "inferior" suffers injustice and often practices self-rejection. As long as gender assumptions are projected onto the God of faith, the patriarchal hierarchy will continue. God is male and male is God.

An understanding of the traditional images of God requires a consideration of the powerful influences that have made traditional religion what it is today. Institutional religion has been and still is pervasively male-dominated. Concerned women are passionately working to both deconstruct and reconstruct religious institutions. In deconstructing, they point out glaring injustices and inadequacies in theology and in church structure—from exclusive male language to the exclusion of women from ordained ministry, from demeaning sexist attitudes to the unequal treatment of women clergy. In reconstructing, women offer creative new possibilities for both church governance and congregational worship. What is found inadequate or unjust is replaced by ideas and practices that are inclusive, adequate, and just. Feminist and womanist (African-American woman theologians seeking justice) biblical theologians offer reinterpretations of biblical texts. Historians uncover the hidden history of women. Psychologists develop new theories and practices that attend to the strengths and needs of women. The goal of Jewish and Christian feminists/womanists involved in this effort is to help create a community of equals that will be marked by radically inclusive spiritual nurture, worship, and presence in the world. Recognizing the pervasiveness of oppression in a patriarchal system, women seek a broad reconstruction. Leading feminists/womanists have joined with many voices in sounding the major theme of justice: gender justice, racial justice, sexual lifestyle justice, social justice, international justice.

This exploration into traditional and expanded images of Deity focuses on gender justice. More specifically, the goal is to understand the relationship between God images and a woman's self-image and self esteem.

Part of the power of my experience at Delphi was the

thrilling sense that women's lives were qualitatively different in the ancient past. Many women want to believe
that there was a society in which women were self-
defined and respected, a society in which women lived
freely and fully as men's equals. Feminist/womanist an-
thropologists, psychologists, and theologians encourage
women to recognize that indeed they do have such a
history.[6] In Delphi the conviction that there was indeed a
prepatriarchal society filled my being.

An analysis of physical evidence found in burial places
and other ruins points to an early European society in
which women were equal to men in most aspects of their
daily lives. Women were even envied by men because of
their powerful ability to give birth and nourish their
young. There *was* a shrine to Earth Mother Ge where
worshiping women knew their power and beauty. There
is evidence that in the Stone Age, the first known period
of prehistoric culture in which stone tools were used,
women were seen as images of Deity. This was a peaceful, art-loving culture, with a down-to-earth symbol system focused on land and sea. The shift that came
sometime between 4500 and 4000 B.C.E. was a switch to
a warlike, mobile culture, indifferent to art, with a more
abstract symbol system that was focused on the sky.[7]

One theorist suggests that patriarchy was born when
men's awe of women "turned to envy, resentment, and
fear."[8] Deprived of a womb that bore life and breasts that
nourished the young, men chose to control the power of
women, especially the reproductive power of women.
(Perhaps this male envy of women is the envy that Freud
reinterpreted as penis envy.)

The establishment of patriarchy did not happen all at
once. Gerda Lerner suggests that its development was a
process that evolved over nearly twenty-five hundred
years, starting as early as 3100 B.C.E. and ending around
600 B.C.E. Some trace its beginnings to the shift from a
hunting and food-gathering society to an agricultural society. When lands were needed for planting and still later
for grazing herds of animals, the concept of private prop-

erty developed. With private property came the exercise of physical struggle and force to secure the land.[9] When the accumulation and protection of private property becomes essential to one's security, those seeking such protection need to amass a sizeable family as well as abundant material assets in order to establish themselves within their community. In many societies only men were permitted to possess property. Establishing themselves required that they claim dominion over their families. A man's goal of establishing dominion over women and children was complicated by the fact that he might not be sure who his children were. The maternity of a child is self-evident; paternity can be uncertain. Men had to be confident that "their" wives were producing only "their" children. With private property, then, kinship arrangements shifted. One's heritage was traced through the father's line, not the mother's, and males dominated and controlled women's sexuality and reproduction. The dominion of men over women became universal. As Lerner points out, "There is not a single society known where women-as-a-group have decision-making power *over* men or where they define the rules of sexual conduct or control marriage exchanges."[10]

It is not difficult to envision the sequence of events in the shift from an egalitarian to a patriarchal society. Each man sets out to secure his private property. The more human beings he "owns," the more productive he can be as farmer, herdsman, or craftsman. Surely women and children become most important items among a man's possessions. He takes over the sexual rights of his woman or women in order to know what is "rightfully" his. Thus patriarchy becomes established in individual families in which father is lord and decision-maker.

The individual father-lords compete for recognition as patriarch of clan or society. Within the clan, men begin to want what other men have. They fight for it. If they want what those outside the clan possess, they go to war. The warriors learn that in order to take over other groups, they need only capture the children. The mothers will submit to their captors' demands in order to save their children from harm. Women become slaves to men.[11]

An additional factor contributing to the domination of women by men is biology. Men can conquer women and children because they are stronger and larger; they can and do overpower women. Comparatively, male bodies have more muscle; female bodies, more fatty tissue.

Thus economic conditions, sociological factors, psychological experience, and biological differences combine to make the emergence of patriarchy possible.

Of central significance to a woman's self esteem is the shift that coincided with the rise of patriarchy, namely the shift from polytheistic gods and goddesses to a monotheistic Deity represented predominantly in patriarchal terms. Goddess worship continued long after the subordination of women to men in most aspects of their lives. However, Lerner writes, the goddesses could not break patriarchy. "The symbolic devaluing of women in relation to the divine becomes one of the founding metaphors of Western civilization."[12]

The powers of creation and fertility were transferred from the Goddess to God. In the process the ancient Goddess who was perceived as one supreme life force with different manifestations, reflecting the culture in which she was worshiped, was fragmented into myriad goddesses. Even the goddesses who survived were transformed from life-giving deities connected with birth, death, and rebirth to warrior deities who interceded with the dominant male God.[13] Just as females became subordinate to males, the goddesses were replaced first by the gods, then by God.

Hebrew monotheism wiped out the fertility goddesses and ascribed both creativity and procreativity to a male God, Yahweh, Lord and King, who creates without a female counterpart. (In one of the three narrative sources that make up the creation story, Deity transcends all images and is not able even to be named.)

The book of Genesis records that the monotheistic God who creates humankind then gives the power of naming to man. Seeing woman, the man exclaims: "This at last is bone from my bones, and flesh from my flesh! This is to be called woman, for this was taken from man" (Gen. 2:23). Lerner's comment:

> The naming here not only is a symbolic act of creativity, but it defines Woman in a very special way as a 'natural' part of man, flesh of his flesh, in a relationship which is a peculiar inversion of the only human relationship for which such a statement can be made, namely, the relationship of mother to child.[14]

While there are female images of Deity in the Hebrew scriptures—God imaged as mother (Isa. 66:13), as a woman giving birth (Isa. 42:14), as midwife (Ps. 22:9), as mother bird (Luke 13:34), as the female personification of Wisdom (Wisd. Sol. 6–8)—these images have been eclipsed by the dominant male imagery.

Understandably, the achievement of monotheism set people free from the bloodshed that took place among warring clans in the name of warring deities, as well as from the human sacrifice that was a part of individual theologies. Monotheism asserts one Deity, creator of all people and at war with none. The insight I enjoyed at Delphi when I felt the affirming power of Goddess, experienced soundly as female spirit, was that monotheism as we have known it has distorted and reduced our awareness of the mystery of Deity in our lives. The distortion and reduction has been especially harmful to women. Monotheism as we have known it has primarily meant the worship of a male God. Yet everyone needs to discover her or his unique expression of the Deity, and many women are conscious that the traditional images of a male God in the Christian churches block that discovery.

Traditional Images of God in the Christian Church

Worship in almost any congregation of any Christian denomination is addressed primarily to Father God, secondarily to Lord Jesus Christ. Both images are powerful; both images are exclusively male and perpetuate a male hierarchy. The third image, Spirit God, sometimes imagined as female, sometimes male, and often as genderless, generally takes a weak third place in Christian worship.

God as Father

Father God is a powerful image that conveys to many men and women that God is close, involved, caring, and attentive. Father God also matches the specific needs of many individuals. One of the reasons the image of God as Father is so appealing is that patriarchal society has generally kept fathers both out of touch with their legitimate feelings and removed from their children's emotional needs. As adults, many men and women describe their early relationships with their fathers as weak, their fathers as absent or distant. And yet unless they have been seriously damaged by a natural father, everyone wants a nurturing and loving father who is present and close. Father God helps fill that need.

Males, whether potential or actual fathers, find a reflection of themselves in Father God. (In the Roman Catholic Church, in which clergy are still denied marriage, the priests become spiritual "Fathers." Anglican and orthodox clergy*men* are also spiritual "Fathers." Episcopalians are struggling to find an acceptable title for ordained women priests. When I raised the question with a woman priest colleague, she said she is glad that she has a higher degree and can be called "Doctor." One person in her congregation, obviously unsettled by women priests, recently called her "Father" after a service. "Mother" is neither the title most women priests desire nor a title the members of their congregations choose to give them. One hopes that the presence of clergywomen will help all of us recognize that adults more appropriately need spiritual sisters and brothers, not fathers and mothers.)

Some women and men who had good enough fathering and cherish their natural fathers are able to project Father Godliness onto them and at the same time project their good paternal experience onto Father God. God is like father and father is like God. Some women and men who did not experience a present, intimate father are often drawn to Loving Father God, an all-powerful figure who provides remedial parenting. Some of those who were abused by punitive natural fathers may feel they are able to make up for that deprivation by turning to a protective, loving Father God.

Women generally have more varied reactions to Father God. A growing number of them are absolutely unable to relate to Father God imagery which they experience as exclusive, unjust, and a magnification of the dominance of male authority that surrounds them. Women who were abandoned or abused by their fathers move in either direction with regard to Father God imagery. Some find solace and are passionately attached to the concept of protective Father God who replaces their abusive natural fathers. Others refuse to consider God to be anything resembling their earthly fathers; they seek a more appropriate symbol of Deity or reject God altogether.

Some women are as attached to Father God imagery as they are to their caring fathers. God is like father and father is like God. Yet Father God imagery that is not balanced by Mother God gives a clear message of the ascendancy of father over mother. God is also presented as a dominant adult in authority over his submissive children. While men may see themselves like the Father as well as a son of the Father, women can see themselves only as children of this Father.

Two major reasons that it is so difficult to balance Father God with more inclusive symbols of Deity in worship are that the metaphor has been mistaken for reality and that Jesus called God "Abba."

In her award-winning book *Models of God*, Sallie McFague calls a metaphor "a word or phrase used *in*appropriately . . . an attempt to speak about what we do not know in terms of what we do know. . . . Metaphor always has the character of 'is' and 'is not.' "[15] The word father was used "*in*appropriately" to describe the Deity whom we can know only through symbols. What is known through the ordinary human experience of "father" points to what is not known: the Holy One who creates the universe. However, through the overuse of one metaphor coupled with the underutilization of other metaphors, "Father" has come to be equated with the mystery that it was meant to describe but partially. The metaphor has lost its "is not" character. "God *is* Father," and for many people the discussion ends there.

A second reason the metaphor has become frozen is that Jesus is reported to have called God "Abba," an affectionate term closer to "Daddy" than "Father."[16] From early Christian times, followers of Jesus have repeated the prayer that tradition tells us Jesus taught us to pray. When Jesus called God "Abba," he used a term that connotes familiarity, warmth, and respect. Because he lived in a religious community with people who dared not assign any name to the transcendent Holy One, Jesus' language was undoubtedly met with shock and resistance. Another reason that his God title would lead to dismay was that many patriarchs within his society vied for authority over others. In using the term *abba* Jesus was saying that we have only one "patriarch" and "he" is our author and authority. As Rosemary Ruether reminds us, "Abba" replaces the hierarchal patriarchal family with a community of equal sisters and brothers.[17]

One might wonder if the image of Mother would have done the same. It would not have happened in a patriarchal society where women were the property of men and lacked authority outside the home. Yet if familiarity, warmth, and respect is what is most essential, it makes no sense to denigrate the female form of the familiar title Jesus used of God. God is as close and caring as a parent: like a father, like a mother.

Jesus as God

At the center and turning point of Mark's gospel, Jesus asks the question, "Who do you say I am?" (8:29). While

Christians might answer the question in terms of what their tradition has said about the identity of Jesus, each believer must answer that question for herself or himself, and answer it over and over as our language and theological understandings evolve.

My answer is that Jesus showed us what it is to be human. Central to his revelation was an ongoing awareness of the pervasive presence of God in all aspects of human life. Jesus was God-centered through and through. He never intended to focus on himself (and surely not on his male anatomy nor on the color of his skin) but on the Love that creates and suffers with the universe. His humanity revealed the holiness of every human being. Jesus disclosed what it means to belong to the human community of women and men: to be in relationship, to be passionate about life, to discover one's true self, to be faithful to a vision of justice even when such fidelity meant suffering and death, to be loved and cherished by the Holy One, to live that love through identification with and celebration within community.

As far as the maleness of Jesus is concerned, the simple and sad truth is that a patriarchal world would not have heard the justice message which Jesus' life embodied had the messenger been in female form. The patriarchal world was and often still is blind to female revelation of divinity. Perhaps the maleness of Jesus came down to the fact that women could receive revelation through a man while men would not respond to the same revelation through a woman. How might society respond to Jesse, the daughter of Mary: perfect in Divinity, perfect in womanhood, truly Divine and truly human? The daughter of Mary telling humankind that humans too are divine? (Riane Eisler asks a question that can be useful when one brainstorms about images of Deity: What if the central image of Christianity were a woman giving birth rather than a man dying on the cross?[18])

The word *tragedy* does not seem too strong when one reflects on what some parts of the patriarchal church have done with the maleness of Jesus. A person who gave his life rather than abandon his commitment to a God-focused community of women and men is used by male supremacists in the Christian churches to preserve an all-male clergy. This legitimates the continuation of a patriarchal ordering of men over women.

The images one holds of Jesus and of the Father God of Jesus are dramatically shaped by how one understands the crucifixion. In a remarkable essay titled "For God So Loved the World?" Joanne Carlson Brown and Rebecca Parker review the traditional theories of atonement, all of which claim the suffering and death of Jesus to be necessary for the salvation of humankind from sin.[19] To say that a good and loving God chose to inflict suffering on his (motherless) son in order to right a wrong that had been done to God is to paint a picture of a tyrannical victimizer who must punish in order to be satisfied. Brown and Parker call this "divine child abuse . . . paraded as salvific."[20]

Surely Jesus had to die—he was human. But God did not send Jesus as an offering, nor did Jesus have to undergo the tragic death he faced at the hands of people who rejected the God he preached and rejected his vision of an egalitarian society. Jesus was passionate about justice and love. The message he proclaimed meant serious social change. People who write the rules and control the resources of a society do not welcome change when it means giving up power. Yet Jesus persisted in proclaiming a need for social change. He announced a "kingdom" in which rulers became the servants of all. (Many women find the word *servant* unhelpful because it reinforces the role women have been assigned as domestic, cook, maid, or nurse. Yet if rulers were truly servants within their communities, that is, if their agenda was to meet the needs of the most needy as well as the needs of the well situated, the word *servant* might be recovered. "Servant" would no longer be a patriarchal word, but a symbol of one who cares for her or his neighbor.) Jesus' life and death demonstrated his faith that every human being is worthy of respect, love, and concern. Jesus pronounced the divine commandment of love of God and self and neighbor the only law one needs to live by, and if he had to, he was willing to die for it. Far from seeing self-love as incompatible with God-love, he saw the close connection between love of God and love of self and love of neighbor. Self esteem resembles esteem for God.

> [Jesus said:] You must love the Lord *your God* with all your heart, with all your soul, and with all your mind. This is the greatest and the first commandment. The second resembles it: You must love *your neighbour* as *yourself*. On these two commandments hang the whole Law, and the Prophets also (Matt. 22:37–40, emphasis added).

Feminists such as Brown and Parker welcome new theological positions that hold that God suffers in solidarity with those who suffer, not because suffering is intrinsically redemptive; relationship and solidarity are redemptive. The cross of Jesus is positive because Jesus' solidarity with those in sorrow and pain is positive. A Christianity true to a God of love is essentially based on justice, radical love, and liberation, not on the glorification of suffering.

Rita Nakashima Brock, a feminist theologian writing about Christology, refers to Christ as the Christa/community. She deliberately uses the female word *Christa* to highlight her belief that the term *Christ* points not only to a male Jesus who founded the first Christian community, but to the women and men who made up that community and continue to function as the Christa/community today. Jesus was a central part of that community, but only a part of a core group.[21] At first glance this may sound like a radical distortion of traditional Christian faith; rather, it is a shift in focus. The creed of the Christian churches professes faith in God, Jesus Christ, Holy Spirit, the church catholic, and the communion of saints. Brock has placed the spotlight on the community, and essentially a Christa/community—which is to say the communion of saints.

In John's Gospel, Jesus provides the transition from his

earthly life, that of a God-centered man who revealed what it is to be human, to a time when his followers would look less to him than to the Spirit or Advocate for a sense of the Holy: " . . . because unless I go, the Advocate will not come to you" (John 16:7). Women might take consolation in this passage. Jesus himself pointed beyond the Son God to the inclusive Spirit.[22]

God as Spirit

As a child I often puzzled over how the Holy Spirit could maintain a separable personhood within the Trinity. The Spirit was either the Spirit of God or the Spirit of Jesus. One could turn to the Spirit as a convenient word for describing the mysterious link between Father and Son. Yet it was difficult to figure out what was going on in the intimate relationships among these three in one. At the same time the image of "breath of the Holy Spirit" was expansive and attractive. When I needed inspiration my prayer began "Come Holy Spirit." In those moments I knew in my heart a God who was Spirit.

Some perceive the Spirit image as female; others, as male. In any case, God/dess as Spirit has perhaps accumulated less distortion than Father God and remains a powerful image of Deity especially available to women seeking inclusiveness. Holy Spirit might best convey the truth that God/dess "is not" Father/Mother, not Son/Daughter; nor is God/dess any concrete image used to express the inexpressible. Spirit might also best describe the awareness of the constant presence of God/dess in human life, intensely bringing to consciousness the Christian belief that women and men live in a holy universe thoroughly worthy of respect and care.

The Spirit challenges the limits of our human metaphors. Transpersonal Spirit, elemental but present, has been imaged as fire, dove, wind, earthquake, light, breath. Yet in spite of its power to express the inexpressible, the Holy Spirit has been something of a stepchild of the more dominant concepts of Father and Son, concepts that can be more easily visualized.

Toward More Inclusive God Imagery

No single metaphor or image of Deity, nor any combination of images of Deity, is large enough. And yet embodied people seek images or metaphors to express the incomprehensible, mysterious, both transcending and immanent Deity. Better to recognize the Deity in what is known and experienced than to assent only to abstract language that names a power beyond knowing. Like Jesus, and at his invitation, we can find the presence of God in the earth and air and fire and water; in the miracles of nature; in inquisitive minds and loving hearts that meet in relationship; in children's cries and laughter; in adults' tears and moments of ecstasy; in the immediacy of the poor and homeless and the passion of the inspired. We find the one God in the stories of God-with-us revealed in the Hebrew scriptures and in the remarkable life of the prophet Jesus reported through the Gospels. Better that we come to expansive images of a monotheistic Deity than settle for a hierarchical God, Father, Lord, King who dominates our universe and helps patriarchy keep women in a subordinate position. Simply the fact that the male word *God* is still accepted in most parts of our patriarchal culture as a gender-inclusive word, but the female word *Goddess* is deemed pagan, speaks to the distortion of our language and concepts of Deity.

While the incomprehensible Deity is neither male nor female, the first mention of God imagery in the opening book of the Hebrew scriptures is that both male and female human beings *image* God.

In the book of Genesis we read that God created humankind in God's own image; "male and female [God] created them" (Genesis 1:27).

An obvious way to keep alive the scriptural claim that women image Deity is to keep alive a female metaphor of

Deity: "God" refers to male deity; "Goddess," to female deity. Many may yearn for the day when all gender-specific language of Deity will be balanced by symbols of the other gender as well as by powerful genderless images. Meanwhile a growing number of women feel the need for female concepts in order to reclaim the truth that they, too, image the Holy One.

One might consider the church of today an institution living in transitional space. The church is in a painful transition between the use of exclusively or predominantly male language in worship, prayer, and scripture and the emergence of inclusive-language lectionaries, hymnals, and liturgical prayer. (Male-designed liturgy relies almost exclusively on the spoken word; feminist liturgy relies on spontaneity, community engagement, gesture, and symbol as well as the spoken word.) In the transitional space of today's church, an increasing number of women choose Goddess to bring balance to the distorted male imagery. More important, Goddess is transforming women's experience of themselves as woman and of Deity as "womanspirit-filled." To use female language in naming the incomprehensible Deity makes more available a perception of the fullness of the mystery of God. In the process one can recover what has long been hidden: the holiness of women, made in the image of God. Turning to Goddess can trigger an experience with the nurturing, life-giving Deity, accompanied by an overwhelming feeling of vitality and hope. The Holy is made tangible to women in a way that the God word, assumed to be inclusive, could never evoke.

Theologian Carol Christ tells a story in which God and woman change places. As God, the woman hears a still small voice say, "In God is a woman like yourself. She shares your suffering. She, too, has had her power of naming stolen from her. First she was called an idol of the Canaanites, and then she ceased to exist as God."[23]

I know that the word *Goddess* is a stumbling block for many women and perhaps for most men. Patriarchy has successfully degraded the word *Goddess* for many people. But women are empowering women to rediscover the Goddess, and they are doing so with profound results. A woman colleague's story helped me make the leap of faith. She told of her conversion to Goddess when she was trying to conceive a child. Nursing first one child and then the second with and within the Goddess were transforming religious experiences. I shared both my colleague's story and my own with a small seminary class. The following day a new mother was bursting to tell the group what happened to her when she left the campus after the previous session. She admitted that she had been turned off and disturbed by the word *goddess*—she wanted nothing to do with it. Yet alone in her car on her commute back home to care for her baby, she said the "forbidden" word, and she had an intensely vital experience of herself as woman, as nursing mother, as image of Goddess. Women dare to rediscover Goddess in moments of both enormous hesitation and great determination. Each story speaks of the discovery of a new sense of the beauty of woman. (Women readers who want to recover a remarkable symbol of Deity might try prayerfully saying "Goddess" out loud several times, open to the revelation they may experience.) As the feminist theologian Starhawk writes,

> The importance of the Goddess symbol for women cannot be overstressed. The image of the Goddess inspires women to see ourselves as divine, our bodies as sacred, the changing phases of our lives as holy, our aggression as healthy, our anger as purifying, and our power to nurture and create, but also to limit and destroy when necessary, as the very force that sustains all life. Through the Goddess, we can discover our strength, enlighten our minds, own our bodies, and celebrate our emotions. We can move beyond narrow, constricting roles and become whole.[24]

In addition to the need for gender-inclusive images of Deity is the need for more community-conscious concepts that will counter excessively privatized God language and religious practices. Sallie McFague's effort is to use ecologically responsible metaphors of Deity that destabilize all dualisms, level all hierarchies, and include animate and inanimate life as well as all of the created universe. She arrives at the metaphors of the universe as God's body and of God as mother, lover, and friend.[25] If the universe were revered as God's body, one would be less inclined to use the resources of this earth for selfish or mindless purposes and would be more respectful of how God's body is handed on to future generations. If the universe were revered as God's body, everyone might develop a more respectful attitude toward his or her own body, a body that both images God and is part of the body of God.

Images of Deity Important to the Women in This Study

Four of the twenty-one women interviewed in this study have no difficulty with traditional images of God, although one says she does not image God in gender-specific terms. A fifth, Harriet, feels most comfortable relating to God as Father—"the strong, helpful, hold-me-close-and-protect-me father" who reflects her own father.

Harriet was sexually molested by her grandfather and later by several men. While she knew heartbreaking mistreatment in these male relationships, her relationship with her father remained strong and vitally important. Only at age twenty-five, while still in an abusive marriage, did Harriet begin to deal with her homosexuality. During an anguished transition from marriage to a lesbian relationship, her father continued to be understanding and supportive. And Father God continued to be Harriet's Deity. It was out of sensitivity to the lesbian community and to women who find exclusively male God imagery offensive that Harriet was helped to discover new possibilities in God imagery and language. Excited by God concepts she did not intentionally seek, Harriet stays open to new experiences of God at the same time that "Father" remains her cherished image.

For several others in the group, the discovery of female images of Deity has been central to their move to a more positive self-concept.

For example, Amy considers a new sense of her true self to be an integral part of her changing God imagery. Over a ten-year period she became increasingly aware of deep-seated anger she felt toward the male image of God that she had accepted without question from childhood into adult life. One of her first attempts to deal with her anger was to simply repeat the word *God* every time a male pronoun appeared in song or prayer or scriptural text. Then she realized that "God" is as male as "he." She then searched for a genderless, abstract image of Deity but remained dissatisfied.

Through insights she received in her therapy, Amy realized that male God imagery was intricately tied in with her body image. When she began envisioning Deity in female form, she was able to claim her female body as essentially good rather than continue to believe that the male body, reflective of male Deity, was the norm. She could relate the shame she felt about her rounded, full body to her assumption that to be attractive, she should model herself on the straight, slim (male) body.

> I experience a lot of freedom in referring to God as She—and believing it. Believing that I am created in Her image, valuable and good. I can begin to see female as the norm, womanhood as sacred, sexuality as sacred. I'm not angry at Her.

Jeanne has become so sensitive to inclusive God/dess language that she becomes distressed and mute in worship services that use exclusively male language. She finds herself silently arguing, for example, when she reads a traditional confession of faith. Worship becomes work and void of religious experience.

Jane's image of God first shifted from the old white man with a beard to a Spirit God; then she discovered the Goddess.

God was not a dictator or wrathful judge, but a Spirit—
creating, sustaining, and sometimes weeping as we destroy
what we've been given. It didn't dawn on me until the late
seventies that there could be a female spirit . . . I knew and
embraced the femaleness of God. The sense of Goddess and
the sense of the rising of the female power in the church
became very helpful. When I pray I see God in lots of
shapes, places, and ways, but primarily as female. Part of my
whole theology now is belief in the God in each one of us.

Melanie's journey was similar. Her bearded male God
was "a fatherly image who demanded what my parents
had—a list of 'shoulds.' In seminary I found a com-
plement to the Father—the Mother who loved me
unconditionally."

As a child, Brenda developed a close relationship with
the crucified Jesus through her intense participation in
Roman Catholic worship and religious practices. All of
her images of Deity were "male, hierarchical, and frightening." Religion courses in college provided her with a
new world.

I was a dry sponge soaking water. I became hooked on religion. Deity became not "he," but I didn't dare say "she"
until graduate school. . . . Today I don't really have an image. God is a swirling mist with arms. Sometimes the arms
are tender, sometimes strong, but not male or female arms
and the image has no face. I'm afraid to put a face on the
image because that gets too particular.

Kit also attributes her adult interest in religion to college religion courses, specifically about women and religion and feminist ethics. She had received a distorted
image of woman in her family of origin. Having lived the
typical housewife/mother role for twenty years, her
mother (as discussed in chapter 1) went through a mid-
life crisis in which she rejected her female identity and
went in search of a more satisfying way of putting her
life together. The message Kit heard from her mother was
that female identification was neither fulfilling to women
nor valued by society. Then Kit enrolled in the courses in
women's studies.

The classes were eye-opening. I kept a journal on images of God. I don't think I had really thought about it before. It was very helpful to get a sense that you could be freed. Again, it comes back to messages [she had received from her mother] of "nurturing is feminine so you don't want to do that." "Motherhood is also very feminine so you may not want to do that." I found consolation thinking of a God that might be mothering; that almost legitimized some characteristics that I didn't want to deny.

Ginger had no problem with male God imagery until she enrolled in a course about women in religion. Although she primarily relates to God as higher power, she found a female image of Goddess to be comforting and nurturing. "I could relate to her and she could relate to my feelings and thoughts in a way I had not thought of before."

Perhaps none of the women was in greater anguish about God language and God imagery than was Elizabeth. She was assigned to a conservative congregation that had little tolerance for the question of using inclusive language in speaking of humankind and no interest in altering God imagery to include female or genderless concepts of Deity. Elizabeth felt that her position was neither understood nor respected. She reached a point of desperation, concluding that there is no God and that the church "is just a bunch of neurotics." Just prior to our meeting she had lamented to a friend,

I'm going to someday do a Ph.D. dissertation and research relationships between clergy and their fathers, because I really think there's some absenteeism there that's putting them on this continual search for approval by God as a male figure. In some way what's been happening to me is that my God has died. . . . I'm trying very hard now to renegotiate a relationship with God.

Elizabeth then began reading current feminist spirituality. She excitedly fumbled for words to express recent religious experiences.

I honestly feel my entire being switched after reading only a chapter [of Joann Wolski Conn's edited collection, *Women's Spirituality*]. I feel like I have come back to myself again. . . . back to the feeling of being completely whole in who I am. Feelings of ease and peace and companionship—these are new to me. For the first time in life I imagine "call" not as authoritative "you've got to do this," but I imagine it as being feminine in nature. It was as if a friend said, "Come with me. Would you like to go?" And it made me feel completely different. It wasn't demanding. It was like a friend calling and saying, "Hey, let's go." . . . Something about even hearing that in a different way helped me, and yet it really made me cry, too. It was a jolt—this whole new thought.

Linda images God as fire or spirit; she hears God through an inner female voice that is unlike her own. "And when this voice speaks, it always speaks the truth." Her major frustration is in convincing her pastor and the women in her church that inclusive language and the presence of women as coleaders in worship is important. They say it is not. The message Linda heard in their disinterest was that the male presence is sufficient and that women are second-class citizens. Religious practice that treats women as second-class citizens will inevitably undermine the self esteem of women.

Some of the women had no specific image of God. Charlotte cannot use pronouns in speaking of God. She thinks of God as a mystery beyond, but she uses adjectives to make God more tangible: God is creative, soft, strong, and loving.

After a prolonged journey through a major depression that ended in a search for God, Glenda experienced God when she heard the choir sing "Be Still My Soul." God has been "on her shoulder" ever since.

Other women said that the most powerful God word for them is "Love." For Lynn, God/Love is neither father nor mother, "a Deity larger than either and both."

Rosa believes that people can project any particular image they choose on Spirit God. Since the death of her father, she has related to God as Father and finds that father imagery reminds her that God is an intimate part of her life.

Starting with the premise that a pastor is God's representative and therefore should image God, Patricia contrasted her images of a male pastor, an authoritarian figure who tells people what they should do, and her female pastor, a careful listener with a strong sense of herself who demonstrates through her life the high value she places on relationship.

Marian also related images of God to specific strong people in her life: her mother, her grandmother, her spiritual mother, and her great-great-grandfather. Visiting a Roman Catholic church with a school friend introduced her to Mary, another strong woman who imaged God for her. However, her earlier image of God was genderless.

> When I was a youngster and being taught about God by my grandmother, I would ask, "Grandma, where is God?" and she'd say, "Look up." I'd see trees and everything. So as a child the image I always had in my mind was that God was this huge tree. So many times I look up now and I say, "God's face is plentiful. Just look at the trees." That's the first image that I can remember. God is a tree.

Conversations with these women only deepened the conviction that graced my life on the Sacred Way at Delphi: If women are able to develop female images of the Holy One as well as more earthly metaphors of the immanent Deity, they will come to a new understanding of themselves, will develop stronger faith in themselves, and will enjoy decidedly good enough self esteem. Women who have been empowered by other women know the priceless gift of their relationships with women. Women empowered by the Goddess know the wonder of a relationship with a Holy One who is and is not like Woman. In knowing her they discover themselves. In discovering themselves they discover her. This is a restatement of the theology of John Calvin. He opens his *Institutes* with the following assertion: "Without knowledge of self there is no knowledge of God. . . .

Without knowledge of God there is no knowledge of
self."[26] If Calvin were able to recognize that the word
God is a male word, and if he wanted his *Institutes* to
address the other half of humankind, he would need to
add, "Without knowledge of self there is no knowledge
of Goddess . . . without knowledge of Goddess there is
no knowledge of self." Without knowledge of self there
is no self esteem.

The following chapter explores the dynamics of good
enough self esteem, using the women from the research
group to illustrate both the absence and presence of adequate self esteem.

3

Good Enough
Self Esteem

My own experience and that of other women opened me
to myself, to my reality as a woman, and to the Holy
within me. As I touched my own reality, as I listened to
the stories and myths of other women . . . their connectedness with earth, air, fire and water, with roots and an-
cestors and kin—I met the Holy in the revelation of my
own being and She was Loving. . . . In that revelation I
have been able, oh so slowly and painfully, to shed layer
after layer of "clothes"—borrowed or forced upon me—
that hide me from myself.

Madonna Kolbenschlag[1]

Self esteem is a concept used to measure persons'
thoughts and feelings about their *selves*. *Esteem* comes
from the same root word as *estimate,* and, indeed,
women and men estimate or evaluate themselves repeatedly. They form opinions about their bodies, intellects,
talents, behaviors, performances, and their capacity to
develop and sustain intimate relationships. Much of the
ongoing evaluation is automatic and unconscious. Sometimes they turn up the volume of the inner censor and
mumble obscenities at themselves when their achievement is imperfect or a relationship has ended, or when
they simply make a blunder. One hopes the volume of

the inner voice increases, also, when people are gifted with a mutually enriching relationship or satisfied with an accomplishment—ready to celebrate some aspect of their lives.

Self esteem is many-layered and complex. A useful distinction can be made between the self esteem with which an infant springs into childhood—that is, the self esteem that accompanies a child's assurance that she is profoundly accepted, respected, and loved—and the self esteem that grows out of the processes of socialization. This is the difference between foundational self esteem and secondary self esteem. Foundational self esteem is always based on the emerging true self or on authentic expression of feelings, sensations, and needs. Secondary self esteem builds on that foundation. However, when there is little foundational self esteem and there is instead an "as-if personality," a defensive secondary self esteem can be built on the sham foundation of the false or as-if self. Thus, secondary self esteem can be either authentic or counterfeit. When secondary self esteem supports the true self, it is genuine. When secondary self esteem represents an adaptation to the demands of the false self, it is defensive or counterfeit.

Foundational Self Esteem

Most people who work as counselors would probably agree that the most essential ingredient in adult self esteem, the foundation of adult self esteem, is the experience of having been genuinely accepted and cherished as a child. Genuine acceptance leaves the infant free to discover her or his true self. The respected infant does not have to live up to her parents' subtle demands or distort her true feelings by expressing only those emotions that the parents find acceptable. The true self emerges with an expression of the infant's authentic feelings and, later, the child's primitive thoughts, which are heard with respect by the parent(s). The infant must experience, through her own intuitive mode of knowing, that she is valuable and irreplaceable in the eyes of her parent(s) and that the parents are reliable caretakers. Acceptance and love is what allows the infant to trust that the world is a good place, that is, that the infant will be cared for and can sleep and breathe and express feelings and find nourishment in peace. A favorable balance of trust over mistrust is what Erik Erikson establishes as foundational for religious faith.[2]

Such trust is also crucial for the faith in self that makes mature religious faith as well as authentic self esteem possible. Foundational self esteem is the gift an infant receives from good enough parenting. Chapter 1 examined the process whereby the parent-child relationship can lead the child to aspire toward a true rather than false self, built on a solid foundation of parental respect and acceptance and preparing the way for true-self esteem.

The opposite of good enough foundational self esteem is weak foundational self esteem. When a child becomes alienated from her or his own genuine feelings because a parent has signaled that such feelings are unacceptable, and the child has been inundated by the parent's mirrored expectations of how she or he must behave, the child will struggle to conform to a false self that can at best result in false-self esteem. "I will be loved because I will be the good child they want me to be."

Of the twenty-one women in this study, Judy, age twenty-nine, has perhaps been the least able to dismantle the false self that haunts her. She is married, yet in some ways she has never really left home. Her parents continue to pay her rent. More significant, her parents' continuous evaluation of Judy at times leaves her feeling like a worthless failure. She is the youngest child of critical and seemingly unhappy parents—and has always felt like a misfit.

> I've always felt that I don't look good enough. I've gotten the heavy message from society that a woman is supposed to be drop-dead beautiful, and I'm not. And I know that it's wrong to think that I should be. That's another thing: I have a serious split between what I know intellectually and what

I can actualize emotionally. So I know it's wrong to hate myself for not being really tall, blond, and thin, but I do. . . . I should be beautiful, I should be thin, I should be independent. But I'm not any of those things. Also I should be successful, but by now that's so thrown out of the water that even if I could manage to support my own self, that would be considered successful. . . . By now [my parents'] expectations are so low. . . . A lot of times I don't even know what it is that I'm feeling.

Unable to live up to the expectations of her false self, estranged from her genuine feelings, the "experience of aliveness" that invites the true self, Judy's foundational self esteem is dismally low. (Even as these words are being written, however, Judy is on a promising new track that is already increasing her secondary self esteem.)

Ginger acknowledges that she does not see herself as a self-confident person and has long struggled with low self esteem. She describes her father as a person with a bad self-image who was discouraged by his parents from following either of the vocations that most appealed to him: ministry and dance. Instead he has tried a number of professions, at the same time working on his self esteem through reading and listening to self-help tapes—but without much success. Her mother gave up her career as a concert pianist when she married. As an overprotective mother, she is compelled to seek assurance that she is central in the lives of her children. Ginger says the family is emotionally close, to a fault. She has shared with her mother the role of central person within her family, but not without tension. While Ginger has known considerable success in numerous church activities, her weak foundational self esteem undermines the secondary self esteem she has been able to establish.

Secondary Self Esteem

Secondary self esteem achieved through good relationships and the reworking of early ideology can be remedial. That is, weak foundational self esteem can be shored up when an adult is helped through authentic, respectful relationship(s) to recover her lost child or true self. Recovery means validating authentic feelings, sensations, and needs. The result of such confirmation can be good enough true-self esteem. Good enough true-self esteem is realistic and therefore achievable, but it also fluctuates according to personal, relational, and professional circumstances. The loss of a relationship or experiencing failure in one's work will often result in a temporary loss of self esteem. If its foundation is good enough, self esteem will survive the setback.

The shoring up of weak foundational self esteem is complicated by the fact that when a person has become sufficiently alienated from her true self, secondary self esteem may be nothing more than a defensive achievement of false-self esteem. In Judy's case, neither correct weight, "acceptable" physical appearance, nor success according to her parents' measurement will solve her problem of a missing sense of self-worth. That sense of self-worth will come only when she discovers through mutual, respectful relationship that she is intrinsically valuable. Apart from relationship, there is no recovery.

The elements that go into secondary self esteem can be seen as capacities, needs, or values. Humanistic psychologist Abraham Maslow insisted that capacities become authentic, felt needs and that needs are a reflection of a person's values. "Capacities clamor to be used, and cease their clamor only when they *are* used sufficiently. That is to say, capacities are needs, and therefore are intrinsic values as well."[3] In other words, when a person has a gift or capacity for an art or science, that capacity becomes a felt need. The art or science is perceived as of primary value to the person. The elements of secondary self esteem, then, are related to what we are capable of realizing. They can be roughly grouped under six headings: respect, ideology, relationship, competence, vocation/passion, and self-acceptance.[4]

Respect

The first of these, respect, is a continuation of the need of the infant for the respect of the parent. In secondary self esteem, respect that resulted in good enough foundational self esteem must find an echo in the wider world beyond the home. Children (like adults) want and need to feel respected in the eyes of others. If a well-loved child leaves her home to discover that, because of her sex or race or ethnic background, she is considered second class or inferior, she finds it difficult and sometimes impossible to sustain her foundational self esteem.

Two of the African-American women in this study contrasted the messages they received at home about their intrinsic value with the rude awakenings they experienced when they moved into a racist white world.

Rosa, having been repeatedly told by her mother that she was "no better and no worse than anyone else, but as good as the next person," developed an independence and self-assurance that served her well in what she now realizes was a sheltered life within the African-American community. Her foundational self esteem withstands the pain of racism.

> I always felt good about myself—just as far back as I can remember. That's the way my mother brought us up. It's just that different situations make you feel bad and then you do what you have to do to get the feeling back again . . . The situation [within a racist community] was bad, but I never really lost my self esteem.

She has found the racist attitudes of some people in the seminary community to be both depressing and disillusioning. Although she had been exposed to racism in high school, through the media, and through lived experience, she had expectations that Christians preparing to serve the church would demonstrate a heightened respect for others, regardless of race.

Celine recalled her father telling stories about his people in what she now realizes was his attempt to teach her about her African heritage. "He used to call me his little princess Sheba." Celine also lived a protected life within the African-American community. Her first experience of racism came when she was in college. Graduating third in a class of 360, she competed for a scholarship that went to a light-complexioned competitor who was her cousin. Celine was conscious of the level of ability of the other woman, and from Celine's perspective the decision was based on skin color, not on aptitude or academic performance.

After college she worked for a government agency where she faced more blatant racism. A high achiever who did well in her work, Celine (as noted in chapter 1) watched white people she had trained become her supervisors. After seven years "it became clear what the promotion patterns were. Some blacks with master's degrees were clerks." Celine's discouragement at being passed over in favor of white coworkers was heightened by the fact that achievement was consistently held up by her extended family as an ultimate value. She was respected at home and rewarded for her competence and success but labeled second class in the work world and deprived of equal opportunity.

These two examples highlight the pain inflicted when a person is treated without respect. Jessica's story illustrates the empowerment experienced when respect is given. When asked to talk about a time when she felt particularly good about herself, she remembered a job she completed before making the career change that brought her to seminary.

As principal of a school for emotionally disturbed children, she was responsible for overseeing the construction of a new center. She also interviewed applicants for staff positions in the center. She found that friends, former students, and former colleagues were asking to join her team. Although Jessica did not use the word *respect* and in fact said she was not fully aware of all the forces that made that period of time such a powerful experience for her, one senses that she had won the respect and esteem of many people who wanted to be involved in a project under her leadership.

> The combination of seeing something tangible come together and also having friends wanting to be part of that, feeling as if in some way I was able to facilitate that and I could see people being pleased with themselves when they became associated with the program—all that made me feel that things were okay and I was okay. . . . I was just being me. So I don't have a whole lot of words to put to it, except it was a phenomenon where I just went "Oh, wow, what's happening?" and they feel good, and when I see that, I feel really good.

Perhaps everyone has a hard time describing in words the welcome and affirming experience of receiving respect from friends and colleagues. It may be easier to describe painful situations in which one meets with disrespect. When the human body is functioning well, one rarely reflects on the sensations of one's well body parts. However, when a part has been injured, a person is quite conscious of what her or his back or hand or foot is feeling. Yet much can be gained from trying to express in words the experience of respect. Respect is found in the gift of relationship. To acknowledge it is to celebrate relationship and increase the satisfaction found in respectful relationship.

To recognize that everyone is intrinsically worthy of respect and to live according to that value is to shape an ideology conducive to good enough self esteem. Such an ideology is the second component of secondary self esteem.

Ideology

Psychologist Michael R. Jackson[5] points out that few writers have questioned how one's core beliefs about life, one's philosophy of life or ideology, structures self esteem. Jackson is convinced that self esteem is based on what has come to have meaning or value in a person's life, but he holds that people are often unaware of the structures of meaning that influence their self-evaluations. Central to Jackson's understanding of self esteem is the ideology a person has absorbed through ongoing interaction with parents and other significant adults during her or his earliest years.

As noted in chapter 1, an ideology describes a person's general conceptions about the world and her or his place in it. These conceptions implicitly or explicitly contain a philosophy of human nature, gender, and role assumptions, and a set of ideals and values and an idea about how one might realize them. A developed ideology includes a personalized understanding of the rules and norms of society. It also includes the critically important point of how one views oneself and one's place in the scheme of things.

Another way to understand an ideology is to consider what a person values. Expressed values are indicators of an underlying ideology, pointing to what a person believes to be good and true. In other words, the things people choose to do and the things they tend to avoid are all related to their general conception of life and their place in it. Most parents explicitly teach their children a system of ethics or values. Children may learn more by what parents do than by what parents say, more by what their behavior indicates as valuable than by what their explicit teaching expounds to be of value. In fact, parental influence is so great that even when a child resolves not to repeat a particular pattern of behavior that shaped the quality of life within her family of origin, as an adult she may have an extremely difficult struggle in trying to break a well-learned behavior. Children of child abusers and/or substance abusers all too often repeat the abuse in their adult family lives. Fortunately, healthy family patterns become values across generations as well. Children of generative, productive parents are equipped to repeat their parents' behavior patterns within their adult families.

Once the child moves out into larger and larger circles of influence, the family worldview she brings with her will be tested, developed, integrated, and owned or re-placed as the child comes to her own understanding of human life and of society and how she fits into it.

In order to achieve adult maturity, an individual must replace parental guidelines for behavior with an inner system of ethics and values. In other words, one chooses values because they have become part of the fabric of one's life, not because they result in reward rather than punishment. While affirmation from others continues to be important to one's self esteem throughout life, the person with good enough true-self esteem is less depen-dent upon external validation and is able to maintain self-confidence in spite of setbacks and disappointments.

Parents are both the designers and exemplars of an infant's first ideology. Chapter 1 reviewed the crucial im-portance of ideology to the way a child perceives her or his place in the parents' lives and how this perception affects foundational self esteem. An ideology will point a person in one of two general directions: Either the person comes to prize her thoughts and feelings and develops trust in herself, in which case the ideology supports a true self, or the person senses that her feelings and desires are not to be trusted and she therefore pursues the ideas and values that her parent(s) hold up to her, in which case she lives out of a false sense of self.

True-self esteem results when a person is encouraged to express her genuine feelings and desires. False-self es-teem results when a person represses her genuine feel-ings and desires and accomplishes the wants or needs that another holds for her. The individual achieves goals that have not been personally expressed or claimed.

Judy's consciousness of weight, which began when she was seven years old, illustrates the power of the false self. Her father, whom she describes as obsessed with weight, told her that he thought she was too heavy. Judy was angry and chose a hunger strike to get back at her father. She says that this was "the only statement I could make, the only power that I had to protest against that insult and assault on my looks and personality." Her memory tells her that the fast lasted about four days. The message continues in Judy's life: Thin is good; fat is bad.

> Even to this day, my parents still give a lot of approval when I'm thin. Like if I'm about fifteen pounds thinner, they think that's really good, and I'm approved of as a person.

When Judy is thin she feels good about herself, not because of who she is but because she has succeeded (however temporarily) in embodying the value that her parents have placed on being slender. In this case, that value happens to coincide with society's obsession with slenderness.[6] The value of her weight loss will be magnified by the response she will get from friends and acquaintances. Judy will enjoy false-self esteem that makes her feel attractive and acceptable. She may have to lose those same fifteen pounds fifteen times again in her life to defend her false self. She will enjoy true-self esteem only if she names and claims her own values and is able to say that no matter what she weighs, she is a respected and valued person. The values that shape her ideology may or may not include slenderness.

A person can become frozen in a false self, resolved to be the projected individual someone else values. Remaining unaware that she has made herself into the person that another needs and wants, she lives without a sense of her own genuine feelings, wants, and needs—unaware of her oppression. Driven by ground rules from the past that compel her to please, paralyzed by her fears of rejection, she settles for false-self esteem.

Many women are blind to the patriarchal rules and values that dictate their lives. They have successfully been indoctrinated to accept with courage and conviction their nurturing and supportive roles in the home and in society and to look upon feminists as malcontents. They may vigorously defend the ideological system that denies their authority and potential as men's equals. As Jean Baker Miller powerfully puts it: "All forms of oppression encourage people to enlist in their own enslavement."[7]

Thus women will say with sincerity in their voices that they want their husbands to be the heads of their families. They cherish their subordinate position in home and society—although they may deny that it is subordinate. As young adults they may intentionally give up the pursuit of their education or the development of their gifts in order to dedicate themselves to husband and children, and they may endure in their self-sacrificing lifestyles to the end. They may even like being taken for granted by those they serve. Women defined by patriarchy would probably disagree with the assessment that they have achieved a comfortable amount of *false*-self esteem.

A place where women can feel themselves in opposition to other women is in the debate about inclusive language. Many women say they have no problem with male language because for them "men" means men and women; "brothers" includes sisters. They fail to see that to assume that "man" includes "woman" is to support patriarchy's subsuming of and thereby discounting of women. Feminists and womanists, as well as a growing number of others seeking liberating language, are convinced that language shapes the way the world is perceived and that to assume that "man" includes "woman" is to agree that male is the norm.

If a person gets in touch with the discomfort or sadness or anger that underlies a false self, she will realize that false-self esteem is neither lasting nor satisfying. A woman's conversion to the true self often includes a change in the way she values women, beginning with herself. No longer willing or able to see men as the norm and women as men's subordinates, a woman recognizes the dignity and worth of the female body and spirit. She knows that her life is precious and full of potential and that it is her primary responsibility. One could say that the move from the false self to the true self is a matter of naming and claiming one's values. The bondedness of women is magnificently evident in the remarkable empowerment women have given and received among themselves over the last twenty years. An outstanding array of feminist/womanist literature makes new possibilities available to anyone ready to read. Women's studies courses invite women of all ages to dream a new dream. Within caring relationships, support groups, and gatherings of women known as Women-Church,[8] where women share their faith and lives through celebration and worship, women find the vision, motivation, and strength they need to be themselves and to reshape their lives. Women have been women's inspiration and support in the revision of patriarchal ideology. Their new understanding of human life highlights the stunning beauty and value and bondedness of women.

Most of the women in this study have reworked the ideology that pervaded their early family lives. New perceptions of the world and their place in it set their agenda. Most of the women have also gone through major mid-life transitions as a result of their discovery of the religious or spiritual values that drew them away from their previous careers and into the ministry. New values set their agenda.

Earlier sections of this book have included brief presentations of three women at different places in the transformation of their ideologies and the implementation of the revised ideologies. Glenda was able to transform her life by correcting the faulty thinking that set an impossible agenda for her; she no longer had to rescue her alcoholic father and unfulfilled mother. Only after she abandoned her self-defeating goal in life was she able to develop a healthy relationship with a partner. Celine is trying to realize the value of intimacy that was not a strong part of the ideology of success and achievement that determined much of her youth and young adulthood. Kit is struggling with her fear of rejection, working to truly believe that she is a lovable though imperfect woman. At the center of their new ideologies, all three women have put healthy, mutual relationship—the third component of secondary self esteem.

Relationship

To say that good enough self esteem requires positive, intimate relationship is to say something so obvious to a woman that it seems hardly to need articulation. Process philosophers and theologians expound a worldview that is thoroughly relational: everything in the universe is related to every other thing in time and in space, without beginning or end.

To drive home this point I sometimes ask students to define the boundaries of the seminary or of a local church. They can't do it. Similarly, they are unable to tell me when the influences on their lives began. To be true to their nature, human relationships must be understood in a global, open-ended context. Women and men are indeed sisters and brothers who influence one another's lives continuously: what they do and say and fail to do or say; what they eat and drink and wear and the cars they drive; what they hoard and what they share and what they throw away. Everything about human life reverberates. Individuals have an impact on the universe today and the universe of the future precisely because they are relational parts of a whole that is thoroughly interconnected.

Self esteem can be no different. It, too, is deeply relational. The sense of significance essential to self esteem comes only through relationships that are based on mutual respect and acceptance. The expression "best friend," so important to the child and adolescent, points to the need to be the focus of another's attention. Attachment to another is critical as the child discovers herself and her significance.

In this society women have most often been seen as those who carry major responsibility for relationships within the family. In fact, patriarchy requires that women take major responsibility for children and home and family life. Their capacity for intimacy and nurture and the structures men have put in place have resulted in the social expectation that women fill a role, a role that is generally seen as less valuable than the role of their male counterparts.[9] For husband, children, doctor, or executive they become wife, mother, nurse, and secretary. Women have learned to sacrifice their own wants and needs and possibilities to "better serve those they love." In the process women can so lose touch with their abilities that they no longer hear the inner voice that clamors for those capacities to be used—and the capacities remain idle.

A caveat is needed here about the role mothers play in the lives of their children. For some women, parenting children can be a fulfilling (and an exhausting) experience that becomes a passion or primary vocation during a particular time in the family life cycle. They may freely choose not to work outside the home until the children are in school. During years of concentrated child care they might find ways to remain intellectually challenged and socially involved in order to balance the physical and emotional challenges of mothering and remain engaged in the adult world. Yet few families can afford the luxury of one income; most mothers work. In addition, more fathers are sharing in the responsibilities of both child-rearing and housekeeping (though, indeed, studies referred to in chapter 1 indicate that father's "share" tends to be a small one). As a consequence, both parents struggle to balance work within the home and work outside the home. Although the primary parent is most often the mother, fathers sometimes choose to play a central role as well. The decision to devote a phase of one's life to child care bespeaks a person's conviction regarding the crucial significance of the relationship between parent and child.

Women throughout history have known the power of relationships with other women. The power of female peer relationships was illustrated in a conversation with my husband, a prosecuting attorney. He is currently responsible for the state's prosecution of sex offenders whose victims are children. A considerable part of his work is with the victims of these intolerable crimes that devastate the lives of girls and young women and, in some cases, of boys and young men. My husband told me about a meeting in which he tried to prepare a thirteen-year-old girl for the state's prosecution of her uncle. The child claimed that her uncle had raped her when she spent a weekend with him and her aunt in their home. She explained that the first person she had spoken to about the rape was her "best friend." Then she had talked with the mother of her other "best friend."

While details in her story indicate that her first "best friend" is indeed the person she is closest to, she does not use "best friend" as an exclusive title. "Best friend" is another way of saying "someone with whom I have bonded"—the secure connection is what is all-important. This case of betrayal by a trusted uncle highlights the profound significance that trusting peer friendships have for young women who have been violated in evil relationships of dominance and exploitation. Without a relationship wherein she could unburden herself and find support and comfort, this young woman would remain imprisoned, her secret heavy enough to break her heart and her trust forever.

Perhaps it has always been women's relationships with women that have sustained their hope and vitality. Today the bonding with other women takes on new power as women discover their capacity and motivation to change their ideologies, a change that can amount to recreating themselves—that is, moving from a false to a true self.

Women in the study group illustrate the importance of female bonding. Ann calls her women's support group at church her mainstay. Members of the group empowered her through teaching her how to accept support. Amy is challenged and nurtured by a feminist therapist. Jane recalls "Sister Fire 1982," a demonstration by lesbian women from across the country: "To go to that event and see five hundred to a thousand women, only women, and just be in that space where women were being affirmed. . . . " This experience at Sister Fire was a time when Jane's self esteem was particularly high.

Everyone needs a safe place where she can be healed and liberated from her false self. An increasing number of women are discovering this place within women's support groups.

> Without a safe and nurturing environment for remembering, in which we can reexperience the pain of our own distinctive brokenness, be angry, and begin to grieve over our brokenheartedness, we remain lost to ourselves and each other, cut off from the grace that gives us life.[10]

Women have natural gifts for initiating and sustaining life-giving relationships. They have also learned to put others' needs first so consistently that they lose touch with their own capacities. Some women have a tendency to become destructively involved in overdependent or codependent relationships. For example, a woman might minimize her own intrinsic value and shape her life according to the needs of the more valued other who vicariously gives her false self-worth. Such a relationship further alienates her from her true self. Yet from her perspective, she could not live without the relationship—her life has become dependent upon being in relationship with the other.

Recent feminist writers have offered constructive insights into addictive or codependent relationships, helping women understand when relationships turn into self-defeating attachments.[11] A codependent relationship is one in which an individual defines herself primarily in terms of the other person. She has little sense of meaning or value in her own life except that which comes through this relationship, around which she focuses all of her energy. Without the relationship, she would have no sense of herself. For women to come to faith in themselves, their relationships must include both a sense of *attachment to* and *separateness from* the other. That is, a woman must know that she lives only in relationship to others but must not define herself solely in terms of a particular relationship.

When Linda's husband, Richard, had an affair, her immediate reaction was to drop everything and concentrate on pleasing him and thereby winning him back. When Lynn met the man she later married, she changed her life's goals and "concentrated on doing what I could to marry him." This meant finding the shortest training program available that would prepare her to be the breadwinner so that her husband could complete school. Jane believed that her only option was to marry, and not many men had shown an interest in her. Rather than lose the young man who was attracted to her, she put up with infidelity before her marriage and a dominant/subordinate relationship with her husband during their thirteen years of marriage. "The stuff I put up with was part of the training—you don't expect a man to be answerable to a woman. A woman is always answerable to a man." In addition to the need for respect from others, an ideology that highlights women's equality to men, and a sufficient number of positive, mutual relationships, women also need the experience of themselves as competent people who can function adequately in their world.

Competence

Children and adults need confidence in their ability to learn what needs to be learned in order to function competently in their world. The most well loved child will struggle to maintain self esteem if she cannot meet the normal expectations of teachers and other significant adults in her life.[12]

Children with learning disabilities, especially when the problems go undiagnosed, suffer feelings of inferiority and failure. Competence normally includes an ability to perform in the school's recreational and athletic programs, to experience one's body as coordinated and able. When a child suffers from a physical disability, her self esteem will be influenced by the way in which both peers and adults relate to her. She may be perceived as a whole person with abilities that differ from those of her classmates. On the other hand, she might be labeled handicapped or disabled and become isolated from the temporarily able-bodied in the group. If society would recognize that this is a thoroughly relational world, the differently abled might be perceived as sister or brother and the community made more effectively aware that it shares responsibility for the child's well-being.

For children to feel competent, they need encouragement from adults that they have the ability to succeed. Although she had to weigh the mixed messages she received from her parents, Brenda was able to develop an outstanding sense of competence that played a major role in her self esteem. Her father had mostly negative messages about the meaning of life and Brenda's place in it, ready with a list of things a girl cannot do. Her mother countered that theme with strong statements of support, affirming that Brenda could do whatever she chose to do.

And Brenda did. Keenly aware that she had different values from most of her extended family members, Brenda was a straight A student, then Phi Beta Kappa. When Brenda was a teenager her problem seemed to be that she was overly competent. She realized that she was not asked out by boys in her school because she was "too smart." At first her self esteem was shaken by their rejection, but in tenth grade she made a conscious decision that she would not "pander to what they wanted." "If I was smart, I was smart." She has moved through life with a strong sense of her identity as a valuable, competent woman. Brenda can count on one hand her moments of self-doubt.

Ann, intellectually gifted but not affirmed by her parents, was unable to claim those gifts until she discovered herself—a discovery that took place within a group of women at her church. Kit, always a good student as well as a gifted musician, found the "quick fame" she achieved as an oboist hard to accept. "I said to myself that it was just because there weren't other oboists."

A recurring theme in a patriarchal society is women's devaluation of themselves and of other women. Women frequently perceive themselves as less gifted than they are. When a person perceives herself in a dramatically different way from the way she is perceived by others, she suffers what Erik Erikson calls identity confusion.[13] Identity confusion necessarily weakens one's faith in self and self esteem: one is unable to say what self is really there.

Competence is intimately connected with the next component of good enough self esteem: vocation or passion. It is often through the discovery of one's particular competencies that a person feels called or moved to pursue a particular goal or purpose.

Vocation or Passion

A need infrequently mentioned in psychological literature is the need for a sense of purpose or calling that shapes one's life. In studying the life structures of a group of middle-aged men, Daniel Levinson calls this the "Dream." However, the dreams he describes in the lives of the men he studied are primarily ambitions to reach a certain rung on the ladder of success, measured in terms of financial reward or social prestige. My understanding of dream is akin to the concept of vocation or calling, perhaps more accurately described as a passion, something that mobilizes energy and enthusiasm and becomes a positive structure in one's life.[14]

Generally, people do not feel good about themselves if they have not discovered a meaning or purpose that transcends their own wants and needs and personal satisfaction. Such meaning or purpose generally takes different shapes and forms at different phases of a person's life. In other words, the focus of one's passion or vocation can evolve over a lifetime. Children begin dreaming about what they want to be and do when they grow up. Sometimes these dreams are realized and fill a life with direction and purpose. More often the dream or sense of call takes new directions as life progresses. The women in this small sample had been or are now in a variety of fields: school teacher, university professor, music teacher, librarian, nurse, mortician, accountant, retailer, salesperson, secretary, community organizer. Apart from a few of the women interviewed who were not preparing for ministry, all of them came to seminary because they felt that something essential to their happiness was missing. They dreamed new dreams that included the opportunity to develop and express their spiritual and/or religious values. While some of the other components of secondary self esteem were problematic for them, vocation, in this case a passionate desire to be involved in ministry, was clear and strong.

However, a friend who has been important in my life for more than forty years resists the notion that people need to aim at some stated goal or strive for achievement. She says, "The most important thing in life is to enjoy a cup of coffee with your neighbor." Yet her statement in itself is evidence of a passion for mutual relationship, surely a part of a realized dream of this uncommon woman. After her seven children were well along in school, she returned to nursing school and has spent the past ten years working in a hospital. The most rewarding part of her work is relating to patients. Her adult children and their spouses, children, and friends regularly return to the family home where they enjoy remarkably caring and recreative relationships.

Perhaps a sense of vocation or passion is more easily grasped in considering its opposite: meaninglessness and apathy. When nothing seems worth learning or doing or worrying about, a person bogs down in depression and loses all sense of self-worth. Life is experienced as a gigantic burden one faces with little fascination or reward. Helping a person move from apathy to engagement is no small task. The vocation or call may come through the power of respectful listening; it may be heard in the pained voice of a person in need.

Self-Acceptance

The final component of secondary self esteem, which can be realized only when all other components are pres-

ent, is self-acceptance. Self-acceptance is possible because a woman has enjoyed respect within relationship
and has an understanding of her world and her place in
it as a competent, passionate person. The concept of self-
acceptance is close to the concept of self esteem yet dis-
tinguishable enough to warrant separate discussion.

The self-accepting person develops a trust in her inner
experience, a trust that requires a realistic understanding
of herself. That is, she pays attention to what she is feeling, checks out her intuitions and thoughts with friends
she has come to trust, and acts out of her best insights.
Essential to realistic self-understanding is the *acceptance
of one's physiological and psychological givens*: body, mind,
and heritage. "Acceptance" is used here to underscore
that each person must come to a practical, honest recognition and endorsement of her very real embodied givens. The demands of the false self, magnified by society's
conventions, can make such radical self-acceptance extremely difficult.

Ann is too large; Charlotte, too fat; Amy, too well developed. Celine's skin color is too dark; Rosa's, too light.
Terry's hair is too straight; Lynn is not pretty enough.
The litany can go on and on when women allow their
value to be measured according to patriarchal standards.

Studies show that women perceive themselves to be
heavier than they are; men perceive themselves as
lighter. "Slightly underweight men were also the only
group of men who disliked their bodies more than did
similar weight category women." Women were more
likely to have distorted perceptions of their bodies.[15]

Another study found that overall body esteem corre-
lates with self esteem. The nuances of the results are
surprising. While sexual attractiveness and physical condition were related to self esteem, weight dissatisfaction
was not associated with self esteem for women. The
women in this study saw weight as a normative concern
for women. Rather than relate weight with self esteem,
they took weight concern as a given that comes with
being female.[16] A woman needs to come to an acceptance

of her body no matter what measures patriarchal society holds up as desirable.

The struggle for self-acceptance can also be a matter of appreciating intellectual capacities that go beyond what patriarchy deems reasonable for women. Several of the women in my study reported being afraid to let the boys in their schools know how bright they were. They felt they had to hide their gifts in order not to be threatening to males. One became aware that her professional success threatened her husband and found a way to "stay out of the spotlight."

The need for respect, relationship, competence, vocation, and self-acceptance, all within a worldview that affirms women, is complicated by the fact that such needs can be distorted by the false self. In other words, a person who was reared on the conviction that she had to be first in her class and a straight A student to win her father's respect may become an overachiever whose false-self esteem requires a perfect academic performance. A person whose self-acceptance is conditional upon her achieving the body image she believes essential to being perceived as an attractive, desirable woman may become obsessed with her weight and hair and body beautiful. Once again, good enough foundational and secondary self esteem must be based on an understanding and respect for the true self, and for women this almost always means rewriting an ideology. The following chapter discusses more extensively a group of women who have done precisely that.

4

Women Struggling
to Be Themselves

Only the true self can feel real, but the true self . . . must
never comply [with the demands of another].

D. W. Winnicott[1]

The trap that most ensnared the women in this study
was the assumption that if they could be good enough to
win the unqualified approval of another, they would
achieve their goal in life. Being good enough, however,
came to mean achieving perfection. The word *perfect* was
often repeated in the interviews. Only perfect performance would give them the sense of having some control
over the approval they needed from another. After all,
perfection leaves no room for disapproval. As long as one
needs perfection in order to arrive at unqualified approval, one must live in anxiety that the imperfection one
well knows to be part of her life might be discovered.
Feminist therapists Polly Young-Eisendrath and Florence
L. Wiedemann write that they "have never encountered
a woman in therapy who did not believe she was hiding
a secret flaw that others would eventually discover."[2] Ar-
riving at perfection in order to meet with unqualified approval takes a variety of forms for the women in this
study. For one woman, perfection is gained through acceptance by everyone; for another, perfection requires

consistent success in whatever she attempts; for another, perfection necessitates that she have a body other than the one she has; for still another, perfection means making an emotionally wounded parent happy again or saving her parents' troubled marriage. In fact, sixteen of the twenty-one women expressed some form of drive for approval, a drive always related to a false need to comply with the expressed or assumed demands of another.

A second major theme that was evident in this study was gender/sexual abuse. The abuse took several forms: physical sexual abuse, verbal abuse of a woman's (or child's) body, and the psychological and social abuse a lesbian experiences because society does not support what she experiences as her nature, her true self.

The first half of this chapter illustrates that the search for unqualified approval and the damaging effects of gender/sexual abuse best characterize the self-esteem histories of the women in the research group. The second half of the chapter includes more extensive presentations of three women whose stories speak with power of rediscovering woman in a patriarchal society.

Unqualified Approval and Perfectionism

The need for the approval of parents, and in some cases siblings, became evident to a number of the women as soon as they reflected in their interviews on the messages they recalled from childhood about who they were or who they should be. For example, Lynn listed her "shoulds" and added that she felt like a failure throughout childhood and adolescence because she fell short of winning unqualified approval; she was never good enough, never smart enough, never pretty enough to please her father. As a result, Lynn grew up painfully self-conscious, always aware that she didn't measure up.

Ginger, the youngest of four children, sought the approval of her parents and siblings by being constantly concerned about their needs. She took care of everyone. In retrospect, she recognizes that she competed with her mother to be the emotional center of the family. Ginger focused so totally on being responsive to others that her own needs and even her sense of self were often lost in the process. An interesting side effect of Ginger's effort to gain unconditional approval within the family was that although she was the youngest child, she says she cannot remember feeling less than a peer to her siblings. Unlike the more typical youngest child, who feels that she or he can never quite catch up with the older children, Ginger saw herself as an equal player in the family—her secondary self esteem depended upon it.

Super-expectations in any area of life create a false self that blocks genuine self-knowledge and self-acceptance and results in low self esteem. An additional problem with overfocusing on the needs of the other is that the rewards one receives reinforce the false-self process: a super care-giver needs to be needed in order to maintain her false-self identity.[3]

Chapter 1 explored Kit's role as a super care-giver. Kit's need to please became a need to be perfect—both needs contributing to a false self that has made it impossible for Kit to believe she can be loved. She judges herself unlovable because she inevitably fails to live up to her unrealistic expectations.

In the second chapter we discussed Jessica, a woman whose childhood was plagued by a father who expected perfection before he would give approval. Adding inconsistency to impossible expectations, he changed his definition of perfection from day to day. Jessica and her siblings lived in a continuous state of alertness lest they fail to live up to their father's standards and receive whatever abusive punishment he used to convey his disapproval.

Perhaps no one better illustrates the trap of super-expectations than Melanie. Melanie is a thirty-three-year-old white pastor. She recognized several years ago that she was driven to excel in everything she undertook and that she was no longer willing to live with these impossible expectations. Melanie went into therapy. Trying to understand the "shoulds" that ruled her life became a major focus in her self-exploration. The list of what she calls her "all-encompassing shoulds" was long: get good grades; take care of her brothers (although one was only a year younger than Melanie); help with the housework (while the boys enjoy their play outdoors); be loyal to every commitment she makes to anyone ("If you say you're going to do something, then by God you had better do it"); always be a good kid. And Melanie was. At eight years old, she was so rigid about her need to please that she developed a nervous stomach. As a teenager, Melanie began challenging some of the "shoulds," but when she was in high school her parents' relationship went into crisis and Melanie regressed. She assumed that if she were good enough she could save the marriage. Her mother chose Melanie as her confidant, burdening her with details that Melanie kept to herself until she spoke with her parents' counselor when she was twenty. Simply articulating her parents' conflict felt like letting go of an enormous secret and the responsibility that went with it. Melanie remembers the counselor's words, "That was too much for you to bear, wasn't it?" and the relief she felt in admitting that indeed it was.

Yet ten years later, Melanie realized that she was still driven to be perfect. Her earlier need to win the unqualified approval of her parents had become a need to be perfect in all areas of her life—to meet with total approval of others and of herself.

> When I started talking about the way I felt about things, it was always that you had to do everything to your absolute best and there are no excuses. . . . It goes the whole gamut—not just grades. It's how you keep your house, it's how you cook your meals, it's how you take care of yourself, it's everything.

Melanie expressed confusion over the fact that in many areas of her life she feels very confident and free to be herself—academic work, job interviews, professional responsibilities, evaluations, meetings with authority figures. Her secondary self esteem is high. On the other hand, in some situations she is aware of painfully weak self esteem. When she has disappointed or hurt someone, especially someone in the church she serves, she automatically asks herself what she should have done to avoid causing pain. As long as she is under the influence of the false self that demands that she perform perfectly, her self esteem depends upon the agenda of another. She then assumes that "there must be something I can do to make [everyone] happy." The unfinished part of the sentence is "because I must win their approval." While she has made great progress in moving toward a true self, relational problems still reactivate her false self's drive for unconditional approval.

One indication that Melanie has more work to do before she accepts her true, imperfect self was that she often spoke of herself in the second or third person, not as "I." For example, in explaining the difference between her behavior and her brothers' performance, she said, "Melanie was doing all of the things she was supposed to do and more." "Melanie just had to be perfect." "My mother confided in 'her daughter.' " "Melanie had changed."

Her journey, however, seems to have moved in an irreversible direction. She gave examples of recent times when she has intentionally let go of her need to make sure she is performing her responsibilities in a way that will meet with total approval. She has offered more spontaneous leadership and taken more risks in her congregation. At the end of the interview, she said with conviction in her voice, "I really feel very much in touch right now with who I am."

Another woman whose drive for approval resulted in perfectionism is Elizabeth. A thirty-seven-year-old white student pastor, Elizabeth explained that her life was painfully marked by a chronic weight problem. After losing two children at birth, her parents were thrilled when Elizabeth arrived. She remembers feeling that she had special importance in the eyes of her parents. However, she also remembers the conditions they placed on her being truly pleasing to them. Repeatedly, she heard, "You have such a pretty face; if only you would lose weight you would be just perfect."

To compensate for her unacceptable body, Elizabeth set out to win her parents' approval in all other areas of her life: in school, in church, in French club, in choir— "I've been president of everything." Her drive for perfection has continued into adult life.

> I was trying to compensate for not feeling perfect physically, and that is something that you just can't erase. I've been to Weight Watchers. I've read everything about it. It's still an ingrained message.

When Elizabeth was challenged in the interview about her body image—she did not look more than a few pounds overweight—she admitted that she has gained back only eighteen of the sixty pounds she had lost when she separated from her husband three years ago.

> And [my extra weight] bothers me very much. I know it interferes with relationships. It interferes with my work. It interferes. And I know also that when I was rid of it, I felt freer to be who I am, and so I want that state again. My perception of myself goes back, back, back. It's very difficult to overcome. It's still always there.

Ironically, Elizabeth made no effort to lose weight when she lost the sixty pounds. She was in a severe depression over ending her marriage. The depression was triggered in part by a sense of failure and the potential disapproval of family and friends. A divorce brought her face-to-face with her need to win approval in all areas of her life.

The second major theme, abuse, painfully marked the lives of many of these women struggling to be themselves.

Gender/Sexual Abuse: The Antithesis of Respect

Generally when the term *sexual abuse* is applied to the experience of young girls or women, it is used to describe physical violence that has been inflicted on the female body: inappropriate touching, incest, rape, mutilation. In almost all cases the abuse is perpetrated by a man. "Gender abuse" of women describes the domination of women by men that permeates a patriarchal society: social norms and practices that discriminate against women and perpetuate the lack of equality between the sexes in most public and private institutions. The combined term *gender/sexual abuse* includes all of the above and more: more than physical and psychological abuse of a sexual nature, more than the battering of a woman's body, more than the domination of women by men. I use "gender/ sexual abuse" in as broad a context as imaginable in order to emphasize the connectedness of all abuse inflicted on women. *Any denigration of a person's body or gender is a form of sexual abuse.* Insulting words or harmful behavior related to a person's body or gender, especially when the verbal message or inappropriate behavior is directed toward a woman who is in a subordinate position to the male or female offender, is sexual abuse.

A claim is made here that all sexism is sexual abuse. What is generally called sexual abuse would not be as widespread as it is if society did not continue to support the domination of women by men. According to the National Coalition Against Domestic Violence, at least once every fifteen seconds a woman is battered in the United States. This statistic is based on a 1986 report by the Bureau of Justice. The report estimates that 3 to 4 million women are beaten in their homes each year by husbands, ex-husbands, and lovers. That figure includes only those crimes that received police or medical attention. There are more than twelve hundred shelters for battered women in the United States; in 1987 they served more than 375,000 women and their children.[4]

What is missing in a sexist society is a genuine respect for women that does not tolerate mistreatment of the female body or of the female gender.

Chapter 1 emphasized the significance of a child's receiving positive mirroring in relationship to mother and father. Children discover themselves and find their very first sense of how they are perceived by another in the eyes of the centrally important people in their lives. Most often that begins with mother. "How do I look?" becomes a live question in a little girl's imagination when she is very small. Looks continue to haunt children, perhaps most especially during adolescence, when the need for acceptance by peers becomes prominent.

Messages that a child's body does not meet with a parent's approval or with the standards of other significant people in the child's life are heard as strong statements of rejection. To criticize or reject a child's appearance is to tell the child that she should have a body that she does not have—which sends the message that she should be someone she is not. The child can do little or nothing to change her physiological givens. The unconstructive criticism of a female body is an evil that can destroy a young girl's faith in her true self.

Readers may question whether telling a child that she is too tall or too heavy can really be labeled gender/sexual abuse. I believe it can. A boy would not likely hear the message that he is too tall—he might be ridiculed because he is too short. That, too, is a form of gender abuse. What the young girl hears in "too tall" is that something is intrinsically wrong with her female body.

The stories of three women in the research group, Amy, Ann, and Charlotte, illustrate gender/sexual abuse in an enlarged meaning of the term.

The oldest of three children, Amy, forty-five, is a white woman, the mother of two teenagers: a son, nineteen, and daughter, fifteen. She has been married for twenty-four years.

> What I'm working hard on right now is a shame issue. . . .
> The shame issue is one that is about my body. I'm not real
> sure from therapy where all that came in. There were proba-
> bly some specific things that happened in my background,
> not overt abuse so much as messages I absorbed.

Amy explained that she grew up seeing the male body as the norm—straight and slim like her father, who was clearly the center of the family.

Amy believes that she was "fairly free" in accepting her body as a child, enjoying "play and physical feelings like swinging and sliding and moving." Then came adolescence, a "miserable time" of loneliness and alienation, when she discovered she was going to be a woman. She became "detached from [her] physical self." Her physical features and body size are like those of her father's family; her mother is very small and quiet, "tiny and straight." Amy sensed that her mother apologized for the fact that Amy is built like her father, thus increasing Amy's discomfort with her body. She felt that she didn't own her body; it was simply "there for anyone to criticize." She notes that Madison Avenue contributed to her body shame by telling her how she should look: "nice breasts, slim hips—which is not how I looked." Both parents reacted negatively to her emerging adolescent sexuality.

> From both of them the number one fear was sex. There were a lot of messages about not being sexual, and I saw my mother as kind of asexual and my dad as being a little bit confused by my emerging sexuality and needing to distance some. My father's reaction was more damaging than Mother's. I felt very distant from him; there were not even hugs. I saw my sexuality as the cause or fault of that—that's the way I interpreted it.

In response to the suggestion that her sexuality became a split-off aspect of her life, and that her work on body image and shame is a reclaiming of an important part of herself, Amy said,

> What that triggers for me is that in my own journey what I need to bring back is my child's sexuality, that natural sexuality. It's almost as though that's not a part of my reality. People say that children have this natural sense of wonder and exploration about their bodies, and it doesn't click for me. I think I need that for my adult sexuality. That was an important split from my child's natural, good feelings about self. I have a very tolerant husband, and sexuality has bloomed in our marriage. It has been a real gift and has enhanced our marriage a lot.

She writes that what has been transforming for her "is to find that I can take off my clothes and still be okay! This sounds like the opposite of the Adam and Eve story." Amy concludes,

> The old stuff exists in layers. I dig out a little bit, go to something else, and here it comes again. I've gotten rid of a lot of unwanted stuff, but at the bottom is a stubborn layer of shame. When I really feel okay about being a woman and having this body, then I will be free. It's worth working on.

A second woman who was damaged by negative messages about her physiological makeup was Ann, a forty-year-old white woman, the mother of two children from different marriages. The message Ann received from her family was that she didn't quite make it: "I was really neat but there was something wrong. I wasn't good enough." She was tall and pretty, but too heavy—not quite the model figure. At school her height made her self-conscious and, as she perceived it, caused her distress. She remembers being devastated by her second-grade teacher, who singled her out as one of the best dancers in the rehearsal but at the same time did not allow her to dance in the second-grade maypole dance. Instead, she was told to hold the pole because she was too tall for the group. Height and weight became a body-shame problem with which Ann struggled until a very recent turning point.

After twenty-five years of dieting, she was able to come to a genuine acceptance of her body as she approached her fortieth birthday. This birthday was particularly significant because an aunt who gave Ann the attention and sense of significance she did not receive from her parents had said for years that "at forty they ought to take out a gun and shoot us." Ann's aunt had an intense fear of aging, claiming that after forty life was not worth much. As forty approached, Ann starting looking hard at her life.

> Okay, I'm not perfect, but the sky hasn't fallen and my life is better than it's ever been, so I can let go of some of that

stuff. . . . Finally after all these years I have come to believe that in retrospect I was fine. I was very self-rejecting and self-abusive.

Today she finds herself attending to diet out of interest in her health and in order to change unhealthy habits. She refrains from overeating when she is anxious, not because there is something intrinsically wrong with her body but because she wants to maintain good health. Ann recognizes the no-win conflict that her ideology contained.

> Even if I lost all the weight I could, I'd still be too tall. I'd still not be the model. I still wouldn't be the 5′ 7″ with blonde hair. I'd still have wide hips.

She adds that her mother had a very similar body with which she was always unhappy.

In the case of Charlotte, childhood and adolescent body shame left her vulnerable for the devastating sexual abuse from which she is only now recovering. The third of five children, Charlotte is a thirty-one-year-old white woman whose divorce was final shortly after our interview. She had been married for six years; she and her husband lived together for several years prior to their marriage. Charlotte has no children.

From early childhood Charlotte carried an image of herself as "a fat kid who didn't measure up." While Charlotte described her parents as primarily supportive, what she reveals about her early self-image indicates marginally good enough foundational self esteem that resulted from her primary relationships with mother and father. In adolescence, Charlotte's poor body image worsened.

> I thought I wasn't a normal female. I felt like a different sex or a different breed altogether. I wasn't a cheerleader . . . didn't wear cute trendy clothes, but I wasn't a boy either. I didn't fit. I took that message in from the norm that was out there in society. My sisters fit in girls' roles better. I felt isolated. My sisters said I should be thin and quiet and passive. I wasn't any of those.

In retrospect, Charlotte recognizes that at her heaviest, which was when she was in college, she was about thirty pounds overweight. Today she is very careful about what she eats. "I'm not overweight but I'll never look like a model. And that's okay." She describes her weight loss this way: "Each layer that went away gave me the opportunity to get to know another part of myself." Her weight functioned to keep her isolated from her gender identification and her sexuality.

In tension with her poor body image and lack of positive gender identification was the message she heard from her parents and from her church: "Everyone has worth: your outer image is only a shadow of the person inside." The messages Charlotte received from teachers strengthened the positive affirmation of her parents: "You are a competent, solid student." From grade school through graduate school, Charlotte has repeatedly made strong, positive connections with teachers. Church, too, was a significant place where she received affirmative messages about herself and her abilities. These supportive messages gave balance to her image of herself. Yet because she continued to perceive herself as a physically deficient female, she compensated by seeking affirmation of her intelligence, and she wanted this first from men.

> For years I wrote in my journal that the world is a shallow place—people just notice your looks. But my inner life was rich. I was rooted in it for my very survival.

In the midst of her adolescent struggle, Charlotte lived through a traumatic experience that did unspeakable violence to her inner life. She was sixteen, with sisters nineteen, eighteen, and fifteen—all of whom she perceived as more attractive, more "feminine" than herself. At perhaps the height of her experience of alienation from her sexuality, painfully vulnerable, she was seduced and repeatedly abused sexually by her youth minister.

> This was devastating. My first sexual relationship, the first time I was responded to by a man as a sexual being. It was

loaded in every way. I thought maybe that's what adults did. I thought his wife must have known.

Over a period of a year, the minister frequently asked Charlotte to baby-sit his young child. When he drove her back to her house, he used her sexually. She has lost many of the details of what happened, but not the impact. "I had this private, quiet, not-to-be-talked-about, totally disgusting thing going on." Eventually she was able to tell her sister; the next person she revealed her secret to was Paul, the man she married. After that, the secret stayed hidden for years. (Since the interview, and after working further on this issue in her therapy, Charlotte was finally able to reveal her secret to her parents. She said she let go a heavy burden when she told them that she was the victim of sexual abuse at the hands of a minister they respected and trusted.)

Charlotte and Paul developed an asexual relationship that was built on a comfortable friendship. Although they consummated the marriage, physical intimacy was not a usual part of their life together. Charlotte knew her marriage was not normal and blamed herself. "Am I attractive? For me it's not just sex but being able to reveal yourself to someone so completely." As Charlotte changed during her six-year marriage, gradually discovering herself as woman and reclaiming her long-repressed sexual needs, the marriage became more conflicted. Paul was not ready to change (from Charlotte's perspective, not "able" to change). After Charlotte and Paul worked in both individual and couple therapy, they chose to separate.

> The decision to leave the marriage was really a statement that I deserved more. My separation was a liberation from a whole persona I felt gripped by. Dating, getting back to that whole structure . . . living what I had never lived, what normal people in high school live. I feel that I have such a skewed history in the whole area of sexuality. Since the separation my life's been wonderful. I have been affirmed as a woman.

Charlotte's motivation to begin to deal with the sexual abuse she had largely kept hidden for half her lifetime came as an unexpected gift. She listened to Gordon Jackson, a process theologian and pastoral counselor, give an address in the context of a worship service about forgiveness as not forgetting but remembering in a new way. Charlotte was deeply moved. "At every level his words impacted me. Something happened inside. Some transformation happened at that moment." She knew she wanted to work through and move beyond the sexual abuse she had suffered and kept suppressed, which had split off her sexual self in the process. Her journey toward reclaiming herself as sexual began with her bringing up the abuse in therapy, where she says she is still moving toward forgiveness. My sense was that her first major task has been to forgive herself for being powerless to blow the whistle on her abuser, and at the same time to suffer the pain of working through the impact of the betrayal and evil violation she endured by one who claimed to be ordained by God. Charlotte will no longer perpetuate her role as victim by keeping her secret memories in a frozen past. Her work continues.

Assuming from childhood that intellectual and professional achievement would compensate for her lack of a genuinely intimate, sexual relationship, Charlotte strengthened her false self by becoming a competent, successful woman. She describes her current conflict as difficulty in "merging my competent, intelligent self with my soft, juicy, emotional self." She had long assumed that the two could not coexist. Charlotte is the woman who says that using pronouns in reference to Deity does not work for her. Adjectives, however, make God more tangible. God is creative, soft, strong, and loving. Strength and softness—these two aspects of Deity reflect the two sides of Charlotte's emerging true self.

Women like Amy and Ann and Charlotte suffer totally unnecessary gender abuse inflicted by parents, relatives, friends, and acquaintances, as well as by the superficial social values that dictate what is attractive in a woman.

Perhaps the group that suffers most from the dictates of others to conform is lesbians.

The truth is that we do not really know why a vast majority of human beings are oriented toward persons of the other sex for genital sexual fulfillment and a minority toward persons of the same sex. Some within that minority have a double or bisexual orientation. Yet without sufficient knowledge, society and the religious institutions that have become the ethical "spokespersons" for that society have dictated that the majority orientation is what God and nature intended. The orientation of the minority has been labeled unnatural, debased, evil, sinful.

Consider the process outlined in chapter 1 of this study. The mirroring, the modeling, the messages from within the home and beyond the home all reach a consensus: one's true self is a heterosexual self. The infant is immersed within patriarchal society's major story line: boys and girls grow up to be husbands and wives who raise more boys and girls and then become grandfathers and grandmothers. The girls need to attach themselves to boys because the boys are primary persons; the girls, secondary. Gay men are a threat to straight men because straight men assume that one of the "queers" in a gay couple takes the role of a woman. Lesbian women are an abomination to straight men because women are supposed to need men to be complete. As Miriam Greenspan says,

> One of the most radical aspects of lesbianism, and the most threatening aspect for men, is that lesbians choose one another as *primary persons*—in defiance of the cultural message that women are not persons (in the male sense) at all.[5]

Because of everything she or he hears at home and school and church and playground, the homosexual is terrified that something is amiss in her or his psyche and body because she or he is attracted to persons of the same sex. To continue to repress these thoughts and feelings constitutes the repression of the true self and pursuit of the false self.

In a study reported by Bishop John Shelby Spong in his ground-breaking book, *Living in Sin?*, researchers suggest that the brain tells you to whom you are attracted.[6] The study focused on thirty-eight individuals living in the Dominican Republic who trace their ancestry seven generations back to a common ancestor, a woman named Amaranta Ternera, born more than 130 years ago. The thirty-eight individuals lived within twenty-three different families in three separate villages. Each was born and raised as a girl, but at puberty, when the hormone balance in the body dramatically changed, testicles and penis descended. Apparently an insufficiency of testosterone had prevented their male genitalia from developing *in utero*. The "girls" had grown up in a culture that prescribed field work for boys, housework for girls. The more astounding aspect of the study is that after adolescence almost all of the young men were able to appropriate their new gender identity and discover themselves as heterosexual males. Most married and fathered children. Their orientation toward sexual pairing with females, the study suggests, was a function of the brain and in place prior to birth. Nature was stronger than the nurture they received as "female" children. If additional research corroborates the theory that sexual orientation is set prior to birth, how can society continue to label one orientation natural, the other deviant? To label as evil what 7 to 10 percent of the population experiences as natural, namely homosexual orientation, is surely a form of gender/sexual abuse.

One might argue that the example used by Bishop Spong supports heterosexuality. The adolescents in the Dominican Republic study were heterosexual. The fact is that as much as 90 percent of the population is heterosexual. The more important issue, which the study supports, is that sexual orientation may have nothing to do with conscious choice. A homosexual is probably homosexual within her or his mother's womb.

The two lesbian women in this study told anguished stories of their struggles in a society that demeans what they experience as their very nature.

Harriet, a thirty-six-year-old white woman, sensed from childhood that she was different. She tried desperately to be as feminine and ladylike as the "small, dainty, attractive girls" in her class. In high school she continued her attempts to fit in and be liked by the other girls. "I was always on the outside of the cliques. . . . I felt different, but I didn't know what kind of 'different' when I was growing up."

Harriet's sexual identity was dramatically complicated by the fact that she was sexually molested by her grandfather when she was six or seven. "I knew it wasn't right but I didn't know how to stop it, and it felt good for him to touch me and I knew that wasn't right either." When her grandmother and mother became suspicious, they confronted Harriet, leaving her suspecting that his behavior was her fault. (Only years later did her mother tell Harriet that the grandfather had been sexually inappropriate with both her mother and her mother's sisters when they were children.) The stage was set, Harriet explained, for "let's not feel good about Harriet because she's not clean."

At age twenty-five, after continued sexual abuse at the hands of men she dated and the man she married, Harriet was able to identify herself as lesbian. Her mother's reaction was that such an idea was impossible—Harriet had been with several men, which proved she was heterosexual. Her father, less influenced by social norms, was the one who comforted Harriet on the breakup of her first lesbian relationship. Claiming her true self has meant intense struggle, including alcohol abuse, expulsion from school, abusive relationships, and near desperation. Through the miracle of remarkable relationships with a few supportive women, including a therapist, Harriet was able to survive. Today she is "out," living in a "holy union" with her spouse and at peace in the seminary community.

I've made my roads and I know I have even more to make. . . . [Coming out has given me] a chance to accept men, to accept women. It's like you live in a society where you have to fight not to be stepped on all the time, or not to be looked down upon, or to hide what you are, to hide your feelings. To be put into a heterosexual situation where I don't have to hide who I am, and to have the community—I feel that I could ask anybody anything that I wanted to ask them, as long as it was an honest question, and have them answer me honestly without being offended. That's the way I feel. It's a naive feeling; it's a childlike feeling, and I love it and I take advantage of it every chance I get.

The second lesbian in the group is Jane, a forty-three-year-old white woman, the oldest of three children. Gender/sexual abuse and the drive for perfection are hard to untangle in Jane's story. She is a divorced mother of two teenagers, a son and a daughter, who live with their father.

As a child Jane decided that when she grew up she would become a nun. When she realized that the convent was not an option offered by her denomination, she assumed her only alternative was to marry. Most of her significant relationships were with women: peers and teachers, Girl Scouts, and, in college, her friend Margaret.

Contrary to her expectations, Jane did not find her time at a women's college as affirming as she had hoped.

> There was the underlying message that we are here in isolation to prepare ourselves to compete with men. There was a real urgency to be off campus. If you were on campus on the weekend without a date you were shunned as some weirdo. So even at that female place the elusive male was a central figure.

Unaware of her lesbian orientation, Jane did not know how to deal with the fact that she was attracted to Margaret. They both had boyfriends; they both would marry. And they did. Until college Jane had been "remarkably asexual." She had dated very little, developing a relationship in high school with Bill, the man she later married. Theirs was not a sexual relationship until a few days before they were married—Jane was not interested. Bill was a dominant male who expected a subordinate wife. Jane says,

> He was basically a nice person. The stuff I put up with was part of the training—you don't expect a man to be answerable to a woman. A woman is always answerable to a man.

Jane explains that sexual relationships were not important to her because she had learned not to "see" sex. Her first experience of sexual abuse happened when she was five or six. Teenage boys took her into a house, where they fondled her. She repressed the details. At the same time her paternal grandfather was living with her family (he stayed until she was around eight years old). Again, she has few memories of what happened physically, but she knows she was the victim of incest and senses that her grandfather had anal and oral sex with her. None of the abuse was dealt with: "Sex, you didn't see." Sexuality was never discussed in her home. The family was so blind to sex that her sister's pregnancy was not discovered for eight months. "None of us had seen it. There was that much blindness to sex."

In answer to the question about a time when she felt particularly good about herself, Jane described two protest events. The first in significance was the October 1987 gay and lesbian march on Washington.

> Just the feeling that there were hundreds of thousands of us on the streets of Washington. I had no sense of shame at all. It was an incredibly powerful experience. No shame. We went home from the march on the Metro with gays and lesbians holding hands.

The event that ranked second in terms of Jane's discovering her sexuality as positive and raising her self esteem was her experience at "Sister Fire 1982" described in the previous chapter. When asked to speak about self esteem in her present life, she responded that this was a hard time to look at that issue. She is aware that she has been in a faith crisis, angry at the way institutional religions have treated women. She recognizes that she has burdened herself with the same impossible expectations she received at home, demanding too much of herself as a pastor. Jane's ramblings about self esteem and faith were filled with pain and confusion and fear of failure.

> In order to be a pastor, there's a requirement for me to be strong, independent, and the best. And there's this fear of finding that there isn't any best and that I'm not going to be good enough as a human being to be acceptable to God. For me self esteem relates directly to my understanding of grace. . . . I realize that I'm setting myself up as a representative of the strong women in my ancestry. I'm still dealing with that ideology. In my call I'm working to remember that those ideologies are from the past and not from God. . . . My call is not from [that past], but the way I'm responding is. The type of behaviors that my family insisted on . . . lead to competition. As a woman I couldn't possibly be the best. Self esteem for me is part of the image of perfection. Part of that image is not telling [others] what's really happening. Yet the genuine self esteem, the places where I've really felt good—like the march—are just pure grace. . . . I was just there and the grace washed over me. I'm trying to discover that place of grace again, but I'm so angry about what the church has done to women. I have to separate myself from the institutional church and get back to a personal religion with God in the midst of seminary.

Christian lesbians have been either condemned or ignored by the mainstream churches. Some have found a home in the Universal Fellowship of Metropolitan Community Churches, a denomination that serves the gay and lesbian community. Others have joined with heterosexual women who also feel abused by the patriarchal churches to develop ritual and celebration known as Women-Church. Women-Church groups around the country owe their vitality and motivation largely to the presence and passion for justice of the lesbians among them. (See the discussion of Women-Church in chapter 3.)

I am a member of both a traditional congregation and of Women-Church and also participate in community worship at a seminary and visit numerous mainline churches. Women-Church is where I feel most at home. Worshiping God/dess with women in an atmosphere of mutual respect provides a remarkably stimulating, bonding, life-giving experience. Women-Church facilitates the discovery and rediscovery of the beauty of women empowered by the Holy One. Women-Church builds faith in self and self esteem. Participants repeatedly contrast the depth of their experience at Women-Church with the male-dominated, often uninspiring experiences at a majority of the traditional churches. Most members of Women-Church never return to those churches.

The search for unqualified approval and the experience of gender/sexual abuse were the major themes that emerged in interviews with the twenty-one women. These themes and others are evident in the three stories that follow.

Three Women Discovering Their True Selves

In Linda's life gender/sexual abuse and the search for approval intermingle with deprivation, hope, and new possibility. Marian's drive for her mother's approval resulted in Marian's spending years trying to become the family matriarch. Her adult quest for approval has also meant struggling with the expectation of society and of her family that she be a wife and mother. Finally, Patricia gave up the quest to be Superwoman, which she learned from her grandmother, and replaced it with a desire to live a shared life as wife, mother, and minister. The turning point came when Patricia learned to listen.

Linda: From Powerless Woman
to Empowering Woman

Linda, forty-eight, is a white married woman, the mother of two adult daughters. The oldest of four children, Linda was raised in a multigenerational dysfunctional family. According to Linda's account of her family life, both her parents were seriously disturbed psycho-logically. As a result, Linda's life has been complex and at times extremely difficult. In preparation for our inter-view, she wrote pages of anguished notes on messages she received in her childhood about who she was and how she fit in her world. Her writing also expresses an irrepressible hope and joy and a passion for the health and well-being of women.

The first person Linda included in her jottings was a maternal uncle. He became (at her mother's urging, she suspects) a father figure for Linda. "I wonder if my mother encouraged the relationship with Uncle Charlie so that I would put distance between myself and my father." When Charlie fought in World War II, Linda scribbled letters to him, though she hardly knew yet how to hold a pencil. When the war was over, Uncle Charlie returned and Linda was ecstatic. "He was the only man in my life. He took me places—I sat on his lap and drove the car in the country—he was mine." Then Charlie met Dorothy, the woman he was later to marry. Linda was convinced she had lost him. The message she took from this disappointing experience was that "women are self-ish with men, the great prizes." She also concluded that she was unlovable. It was only two years ago that Linda spent time with her uncle and realized that she no longer needed the romanticized image of him that she had kept alive for most of her life.

Her memories of her father are mixed: he was both harsh and loving. He was an elder in his church and later a minister without seminary education. Linda remembers a Sunday when she was whipped with an electric shaver cord for not being ready to leave for church on time. Later that day, she was enjoying time with her father and was taken aside and asked by her mother: "How can you be nice to him after he was so mean to you?" This is only one of several incidents in which Linda's mother tried to turn Linda against her father.

Linda has studied her extended family from a family systems perspective, reflecting on how family members related to one another within the same nuclear group and across generations. She does not think her father ever separated from his family of origin; he remained fused with his parents. (In Murray Bowen's family systems theory, fusion describes a relationship in which an individual or individuals has not differentiated from a parent or parents or developed a separate sense of self. Such people find identity only as an appendage of another person.)[7] Linda's paternal grandmother was born outside marriage to a woman who later married into a socially significant family and had other children. Linda's grandmother was not only a stepchild, but an illegitimate stepchild. The grandmother left her family home at fourteen and married a man who left his family at fifteen. They clung to one another in a fused relationship and repeated the fusion with their children. "My father wanted to have this warm and wonderful wife, but he was still tied to his parents." As a father, he put his wants and needs first, showing little respect for his children. The message she received was that "all men have power."

"Dad left when I was fourteen. I hated him by then and used to pray that he would die. We were poor before he left and poorer yet after." Linda's father remarried and took his second wife to live with his parents; the marriage lasted six months. Meanwhile, Linda took a job moving trays at a hospital for thirty-five cents an hour, working seven days a week whenever she was out of school. She was no longer an honor student.

Linda's mother was not able to function adequately as a single parent. From the start, she was not prepared to be a parent. She loved babies but quickly tired of small children. Her own childhood had been full of pain and loss: she was sexually abused by an uncle when she was a toddler and was sent to live with an aunt when she was ten. Her perception was that her own mother, Linda's grandmother, loved only the boys. The dysfunction continued in Linda's family and plagues her mother's life to this day.

When she was a child, Linda was told by her mother that her father hated her.

> I tried to stay away from the house as much as possible. It was dirty; there was no food. At thirteen I had only one pair of socks and shoes with holes in them patched with cardboard. But I laughed a lot and had good friends. I also cried a lot, but no one knew that.

At seventeen, Linda was hospitalized because the doctor thought she had pneumonia. She was delighted to be in such a pleasant, nurturing, safe environment.

> The hospital was clean. I got attention and three meals a day. After a week I was sent home. It was like going to hell. Mom screaming, no care, dirt. Of course she let me know that my father didn't care enough to visit me. I wanted to have pneumonia and worked hard to get it. I was able to go back to the hospital one week later.

The message she took was that "sickness brings attention. I am unlovable."

Linda noted several instances of sexual abuse. Her mother was raped as an adult when she lived with her husband and children in a motel room. When Linda was molested by a high-school boyfriend and ran home to tell her mother, her mother went into a rage over what had been done to her daughter. She screamed over the phone at the boy's father, "Your son isn't going to use my daughter as an experiment just because my husband left me." The whole football team learned of the incident and, as a group, stopped speaking to Linda. Linda believes that she was more embarrassed and injured by the aftereffects of her mother's rage than by the incident. She later found out that her younger sister Julie had been molested at six but had kept the secret rather than tell her mother. Julie was date raped at seventeen, again keeping her secret. The messages Linda received were these:

> Women are either insane or powerless. Children are powerless. Don't trust anyone. Don't tell your parents if you are

sexually abused or there will be double jeopardy. Hide your feelings. Laugh; don't cry.

One might wonder what kept Linda's hope alive when she grew up in a pathological family and was bombarded by negative messages. There were several positive experiences related to her parents and other supportive people in her life. Linda writes that her mother is a creative woman with a sense of humor who gave Linda a love for art and a passion for music. Her father gave her a love for books and an appreciation for dressing well. He joined and led; Linda joins and leads. Other supportive people were teachers, a next-door neighbor, and a librarian. Linda's grandmother, hard on her daughter but good to her grandchildren, taught Linda social graces. "She was very ladylike, whether she was cleaning someone's home or answering phones in the funeral parlor." Grandmother was also musically talented; Linda is a gifted musician.

In answer to the question about a time in her life when her self esteem was notably high, Linda recalled the family's move from a pleasant, respectable house into a dreary public-housing project. She was eight. She plunked tunes on the piano while the movers removed furniture. When the piano was moved, she stood in front of a mirror and sang to herself. A mover came up from behind and said, "You're really a talented little girl."

At age twenty Linda married Richard, "a man who was everything my mother told me a man should be. He was big; he liked to hunt and fish." At the beginning of the marriage, Linda was repelled by their sexual relationship. Yet the only way she thought she could get Richard's attention was through sex. She adds, "I felt like a prostitute all the time."

Linda's first pregnancy and delivery were far more difficult than she had anticipated.

> Nobody told me what it was going to be like. . . . The experience bothered me so much that I couldn't even watch a nursing program on television or see a program involving a doctor or hospital without being sent into a panic.

In addition she had relational problems with her alcoholic father-in-law and her distressed mother-in-law, who lived together in a physically abusive relationship. When Linda turned to the church for help she was told that the problems were in her mind.

Following the birth of her second child, Linda became agoraphobic: She was unable to be alone in public places without suffering overwhelming anxiety. She also gained weight and developed pneumonia. A doctor prescribed a series of medications to relieve her physical and emotional complaints and then told her there was nothing further he could do for her. However, in the next breath, he did do something that had a life-changing effect on Linda. He told her about his own life, about his illnesses that resulted in his having part of his stomach removed, suggesting that if she didn't find out what was wrong in her life and do something about it, she would go downhill just as he did. "He was sincere and he shared himself, which was a wonderful thing for him to do." He took Linda seriously. He respected her. He helped her see that she was not in touch with her true self. She knew that she had been heard and began to hope again.

Her next healing messenger was a young man who lived with his wife in the apartment above Linda and Richard. Knowing Linda was ill, this young man brought her a book—she has forgotten the title. As she absorbed its pages she became convinced that she was a child of God, that she belonged, that she didn't have to stay sick, and that she needed to get on with her life. "I changed immediately. I read anything I could read. I started getting better." She went to a community college, Richard accompanying her until she was over her agoraphobia. From there, she went to music school. As a student and part-time music teacher, Linda knew immediate success. She had fifty-six piano and guitar students. She was also asked to direct her church choir.

In the midst of these remarkable changes and sixteen years into the marriage (Linda's parents' marriage lasted sixteen years), Richard had an affair. Linda's initial reaction was to drop everything and concentrate on being the perfect wife in order to please Richard.

> But I didn't lose my power. I was aware of what I was doing, and I didn't want to repeat my mother's life. I took a course on positive thinking and went back to music school.

Eager for a sense of significance, Linda practiced her skill at manipulating men, specifically the conductor of the music school. She took on his classes when he was away. He became overly dependent on her to accomplish his work. At the same time he shortchanged her by having long conversations with her over coffee rather than giving her the lessons she was supposed to receive. At that point her therapist insisted that unless she tell the music conductor that she wanted him to make good on the missed lessons, the therapy was over. Linda called her relationship with this therapist her first healthy relationship with a male. Linda continues,

> What's happened over the years is that I've learned to trust myself. I don't see myself as being manipulative. I'm a human being trying to do the best that she can. I have a lot of love for people. . . . Because I trust myself now, I can trust other people.

A significant religious experience continues to shape Linda's life. Every year she tries to take a trip alone— goodbye agoraphobia—and on one occasion, driving through the farm plains of Illinois, she was overwhelmed by beauty.

> I was the tip of the universe at that point, and the whole universe was benefitting from what I saw. And I gathered that all beauty and all selfless love is shared by the whole universe. Now I don't know how that works, but that's my God.

The interview ended with Linda addressing her current level of self esteem. "It's pretty steady and on a good level—actually a little higher than it was before, because I have this feeling most of the time that I can reach out to others."

The African-American women in this study demonstrated a qualitatively different struggle. They did not find their major conflict to be gender-related in terms of women being second-class citizens in their families or communities. All four of them, in fact, were from families in which the women were the stronger sex, within and outside the home. Marian and Patricia have both been overachievers with grandiose expectations—Marian, that she would replace her mother as family matriarch; Patricia, that she could be Superwoman. Their struggles have involved coming to accept themselves as people with limits and with needs that can be met only in mutual relationship.

Marian, the Matriarch

Marian is a forty-four-year-old African-American woman who came to seminary after twenty-three years of working as a church secretary. Over the same twenty-three years she was also employed as a community developer and social worker. At the opening of the session, Marian said she welcomed this opportunity to "put some things in better perspective" as she completes her seminary education. She recognized some of the changes she has made in her life during the four years she has been away from home territory and is both anxious and eager to develop more mutual relationships with her mother, father, and sisters when she returns to their geographical area after graduation. Marian went on to say that she and her mother have been rivals for as long as she can remember.

The first of ten children, Marian was born prematurely and taken from the hospital by her grandmother, with whom she lived until adulthood. Her mother remained hospitalized for a time after Marian's birth and gave birth to a second daughter less than a year later. Marian's mother, an only child, had been raised by her grandmother.

Marian has spent all of her life in a power struggle

with her mother, the dominant authority figure in the family. Marian craved her mother's acceptance and believed that if she could share her mother's power, she might gain that acceptance. Marian often heard from her mother that she was Grandmother's child "because she brought you home from the hospital." But when Marian was at her mother's home on the weekend, she was her mother's daughter, explicitly put in the role of oldest child or "second mother," and frequently rewarded for playing that role. At the time Marian thought she had the best of both worlds.

> And if you look at my grandmother and her behavior, you'll find that we were the same. I lived in her home and saw Mother mostly on weekends. We didn't live that far apart. At home I had responsibility because my sisters were there. My mother seemed to place responsibilities on me. I remember when I was eight years old, I could take care of a young baby just as good as some women could, and that made me feel good. I would tell the girls in my peer group, "You are playing with doll babies. I have a real baby that I'm taking care of."

Marian's grandmother had lived alone since she had separated from her husband when Marian's mother was five. Marian could discuss any personal issue she wanted to with her grandmother. She liked the chance she had to be the special "only child"—"There were just the two of us." She continues,

> I didn't have to worry about making up my bed, or making sure my room was clean, or getting my sisters up and making sure that they were ready, putting clothes together, making sure they washed their hands and faces. At grandmother's house, even to this day, all I do is sit. And my grandmother says, "Do what you want to do." As a child I'd say, "I don't want to do anything. I'm tired. Mother worked me so hard." She'd say, "Take off your shoes." I would take off my shoes and lie around and play.
>
> I remember my grandmother asked me what I would like for her to do for me and I said, "Grandma, everybody I know has a TV, and I'd like to have a TV." So my grand-

mother bought a TV. That was exciting. Everybody said, "Oh, you bought a TV," and grandmother said, "Oh, I'm not interested in it for myself. I'm from the radio generation. I bought it for Marian." When the TV came we had a great celebration.

She was special at Grandmother's and special at her mother's—and she would never lose that specialness because she was the firstborn. At Grandmother's she felt like an only child and always knew that she was cherished. At her mother's she had power over her siblings because her mother never let them forget that Marian was second in command.

Throughout the years her mother bought her gifts for her exemplary performance. She remembers a sister feeling jealous when Marian was given a watch "because I was in charge." The next gift was her first pair of pearl earrings. A sister who asked when she would begin to receive extraordinary gifts was told by their mother, "You're not the oldest; you're not in charge." Yet later in the interview Marian admitted that she felt ambivalent about her role in the family. When called on to do additional duty during the week, which usually meant preparing a meal while her parents were at work, she would complete her tasks and slip out to return to Grandmother's as soon as her mother walked in the door. "She didn't care whether I was there or not as long as the pots were on." That statement was the first indication that Marian felt used by her mother. Her mother was less interested in her as a person than as a dutiful child. Marian's role was to pick up Mother's responsibilities whenever she called for help.

Marian recognizes that, all through the years, she sought to replace her mother. Perhaps she needed to reassure herself that Mother did not reject her. Since her mother "gave her away," Marian needed to assume a mother's role and "mother herself." That way she would be assured of the love and acceptance that she sensed she lost when her mother gave Marian to her grandmother.

I always wanted to be the mother in the family, to the point where I would tell my sisters, "Mother's not here; I'm in charge." . . . When I was fifteen, when my sisters were angry they would refer to me as mother. "Here comes the mother." I thought that was good then, but now, almost thirty years later, I don't want to be seen by my sisters in that mother role. I want to be a sister to them. I also want my sisters to accept me for who I am because right now only one really supports me in my ministry and the others aren't really excited about it. Nor have I been really excited about what they were doing or are doing now.

Throughout the extended family, Marian perceives the women as being stronger than the men. In response to a question about the role of her father in the family, she answered,

My father—he's just there. He's very quiet and really doesn't have that much to do as far as things happening in the family. He likes to hunt and fish and is a member of the American Legion. As long as those activities are going on, it's fine with him. In the house, my mother's the boss. "Whatever your mother says," he would always say, and "My life alone"—meaning, just leave him alone. "Whatever you want to do is fine." When I told him I was going into the ministry, he said, "Fine," and didn't ask me anything else about it. Even to engage in conversation with him—he would always say "Go to your mother. That's women's problems. Go talk to your mother—I'm not interested."

Female domination of the male has passed from generation to generation in Marian's family. She believes that her sisters have ruled the men in their lives to the point where two of them "really suffered in their marriages." She explains,

I have two sisters who were married three times and right now they are single like I am. Because there's no give and take: "What I say goes." That's the kind of home environment that we were reared in; it is also a part of me.

While Marian's extended family lived in a broader patriarchal society, within the family, matriarchy ruled. Just as women suffer the effects of being second-class citizens within patriarchal society, the men in Marian's family are treated as second-class citizens by the women. Only her father stays within a system that subordinates him to women. Men who marry her sisters leave. The sister who was less than a year younger than Marian was murdered by her boyfriend. One wonders if the lack of equality between the women and men in the family prevents them all from enjoying mutually satisfying relationships between the sexes.

After the death of her sister, Marian's devastated mother began to preach a sermon on not yielding power over the home to a man: "This is why your sister is dead, because she let a man rule her house. If she had been in charge she would be alive." Marian thinks that is the only time she and her mother agreed.

> When we were growing up, my mother always said, "I want you to remember this, that you have two bosses in this life at the present time. The first boss is God. The second boss is me. As soon as you turn twenty-one, you have only one boss—God."

While Marian grew up wanting to get married and assuming she would, as the years passed she wondered if she would ever find a person to whom she would want to make such a large and serious commitment. She knew that her mother and possibly her grandmother looked down on her for not marrying. "But I really felt that I could not live up to those vows, so I said no, I wasn't going to get married just to please my mother and grandmother." (At the same time, by not allowing a man to control her, she may well be pleasing her mother.) Marian's resolve that she would not marry and would not apologize for her decision was a turning point in her claiming her true self.

> I would not be getting married just for self or for companionship. I really would be fulfilling what my mother and grandmother, and other members of our family who think like they do, want for me. And that's not good. And then on

the other hand I have suffered a lot because I'm single and don't fit in the mode of society. So my not being married makes me a deviant against my family and against society. Every application you pick up—the first thing they want to know is if you are married or single. If you're eighteen and single nobody looks at it. But I'm forty-four, and they say, "Forty-four?" and they look at it. Body language says this is really terrible. They would much rather me say that I was divorced than to say I never married. . . .

When I met with [a denominational governing group] one of the interviewers said to me, "When are you getting married?" I said "No time in the future. I'm satisfied being single." He looked again and said, "Are you dating anybody?" "No." "Do you plan to date?" "No." "Well, I think that while you're at seminary you should find somebody and start dating because you never know—you might get married. And according to my understanding of ministry, married people do much better in ministry than singles." I just smiled.

Marian's struggle to be matriarch is tied into her conflict over remaining single and not being a mother at all. While she embraced her singleness a few years ago, only recently has she coped with the fact that she will not bear children. She fell into an unanticipated depression following a hysterectomy. After the surgery, women in her church began giving birth in an increased number. Marian found that at the baptisms she was "holding onto the babies for dear life." Every time she held a baby she felt more depressed. Finally, she began reading about the psychological effects of a hysterectomy, got into some counseling, and worked through the depression. Not only has she had to grapple with her family's response to her single life, she has had to contend with their negative response to her call to ordained ministry.

Marian received little support from her family when she decided to enter seminary. Her mother was angry and called the plan "foolishness"; her grandmother "grieved in her heart" that God called Marian "because it's hell in these churches and I don't think I could live through it." When Marian gave her trial sermon, her mother didn't show up. Her grandmother was present, just as she is at all of Marian's special events.

In answer to the question about a time when she felt particularly good about herself, Marian wanted first to describe an experience that stands in contrast to her positive one. The first time she met with a church judicatory regarding her call to ministry, she was voted down by a two-thirds majority. She was deeply discouraged and angry. "That really, really hurt. But I didn't lose heart." Some of those voting against her did not think she would survive ministry. Others thought her decision was an inspiration of the moment related to her work as church secretary, and not a genuine call.

Marian charged ahead and started working on her bachelor's degree. The following year she was evaluated by the same group. Many of the persons who had voted against her heard her trial sermon and changed their vote. "That was really a very high moment for me."

The changes Marian brought up at the opening of the interview center on her style of relating. She began her work as pastor intern believing that this role would give her a great opportunity to do what she had always wanted to do: really be in charge. She was the leader of the church family—at last a matriarch.

> I would come into the meeting with my agenda, and I really wasn't looking for any kind of discussion. This is *my* agenda. I could see that the persons who were present were not interested in what I had to present. So then I began to look at other models of ministry.

Marian talked with her student colleagues who were also working as pastors; she spoke with her home pastor who was trying to implement a model of mutual ministry in his congregation. She determined that she would try a new style of leadership.

> When I held the next meeting, in a matter of fifteen minutes the whole meeting changed. People came forth with ideas; the quiet ones began to talk and tell me their gut-level feelings. People were calling me during the week asking me to

come see them. I also began to be more involved in the community.

Marian began to listen. She finds herself less judgmental, more accepting of both herself and others, more accepted, and more compassionate. This is the changed Marian who visited her family at Christmas.

> I feel that because I have changed, my relationship with my father and my mother and with my sisters and brothers will be different. I'm not the same person. Just to be in my company for three or four days over the holidays was enough for them, especially the youngest ones, to see the change in me. I don't sit in judgment of people like I used to. . . . I'm beginning to accept people just as they are, and I'm really excited that people are accepting me just as I am. . . . I've sat in judgment of my sisters—especially the two that have had three husbands. Every time they would call, I would give them what I thought about the whole situation. . . . When I talk to them [now], I'm doing less talking and more listening. Then they express themselves to me and I see it in a different way. I see that they're not looking to me to be a judge but they look to me to be a sister, somebody with compassion. So through this I'm learning the true meaning of compassion. The gift of compassion is also the gift of grace; it's how God is working in my life.

More significant than establishing mutual relationships with her sisters is Marian's desire to recreate her relationship with her mother. As she expresses the change, a screen between herself and her mother is beginning to open up. Phone conversations are longer and less argumentative. Marian no longer is driven to replace her mother.

For years her grandmother has given Marian the message that she will replace her grandmother as family matriarch. Marian has worried about what might happen were she and her mother to get into a power struggle over family leadership after the death of her protective grandmother. "If Grandmother's no longer present, then who's going to rescue me from this big monster?" she asked.

Today this does not bother me. I have changed. My interest is in being at peace with my mother and my father and my sisters and brothers, and just being a family member.

Marian concluded the session by saying that her self esteem is currently high, largely because she is challenged to change and knows that she has something to give to others. Most important, she does not have to be the matriarch.

Patricia: From Superwoman to Woman

Patricia, a forty-seven-year-old African-American, is an only child. She married as a teenager; her first husband died, leaving Patricia with six children: five sons and one daughter, now ages twenty-three to thirty-two. Patricia did not reveal details about her first marriage. She remarried in 1975. Her parents and grandparents are divorced; she has a distant relationship with her father and never knew her grandfather. At the end of the hour she summed up much of what she had said about her family:

> I come from a family of very strong women. I think that the only way that a male survives in my family is that the male has to be very strong, have a very strong concept of self—or that male gets swallowed up in the process.

Patricia's eighty-year-old maternal grandmother has been a major influence in her life. She describes her grandmother as a forceful, persevering woman with a clear understanding of her values and a strong sense of integrity. Grandmother dropped out of school after the sixth grade when she married at age twelve or thirteen. Her first husband died when she was nineteen and the mother of two daughters. About ten years later she remarried. She soon discovered that she could not conform to her new husband's expectations without compromising her values. Patricia's grandmother then ended the marriage, moved to the country, bought a house, and lived a hard-working but satisfying life as a single parent.

She always felt that a person could be whatever they wanted to be, and [gender] had nothing whatsoever to do with it. . . . She instilled in me that you could learn, you could be what you want to be, go where you want to go, do anything you want to do. And the only person who could stop me was myself. She didn't say I'd be held back because of gender, race, poverty, or any of those things. . . . She didn't let the fact that she was divorced trap her from doing anything. That's different, because in that family we don't believe in divorce. It was always like, you have to have a husband; you've got to have somebody to help you through life. You can't just make it on your own. She was very different. She was respected—a very respected person in the community.

Patricia recognizes that her assertiveness and independence come from her grandmother: "She gave me the push that I'm able to do things, to stick with it: 'Don't give up so easy. You don't have to dwell on the negative all the time.'"

Patricia's story about her current marriage and her decision to enter seminary was essentially a story about the struggle she has undergone in rewriting her ideology and discovering her true self.

Jay and Patricia married in 1975. He became the father of Patricia's six children from her first marriage, then ranging in age from eight to seventeen. Soon after they were married Jay suffered a back injury on the job. He underwent surgery and was unable to work for three years.

Being the strong, take-care person, I pretty well just took charge. I see that now. I just took charge of the whole situation, and that probably didn't make him feel very good, although he was helpless to do much about it because he had really hurt himself.

About the same time, her teenage children were going through stressful struggles "trying to find their identity," and to further complicate the family system, Patricia became preoccupied with a call to ministry in the church.

Then one day from out of the blue (that's Jay's perspective) I say "Guess what? God has called me to the ordained ministry." He's found out that he's not going to be an invalid, that he can support his family. He's just getting ready to find a job—he's all excited about that. It was almost one-upmanship on his good news. And the whole call really consumes a person—or it did me.

Patricia announced that she was quitting her job of nine years in order to go to school full-time. She took her graduate equivalency diploma into the university admissions office and applied for college entrance. After she received an A in her trial course, she signed up as a full-time student. Jay worked full-time; Patricia found part-time work. The home, alive with restless teenagers, was tension-filled, but Patricia was only partially present to the problems as she charged at top speed toward her goal.

It was all very exciting, but I paid the toll because after about [my] third year in school, Jay was just tired and fed up. He felt like he was way down on the list. We never sat down and talked; he never told me how he felt. It's very hard for him to sit down and talk about things that are really bothering him and especially when it has to do with God. Saying no to me was like saying no to God. So he held all that hostility in. My stick-to-itiveness said, "Don't listen to this—you have to do what you have to do." . . . It was just hurt and pain and suspicion and second-guessing, and you can't even begin to talk if you don't trust.

Jay and Patricia thought the marriage was over but decided on a one-year legal separation. Families and friends were baffled by the decision. Distressed and confused, Patricia turned to her woman pastor and found "fantastic support." She explains,

I was very comfortable with her and shared things with her. I don't know how I would have shared them with a male pastor, and somehow she seemed to be able to hear the hurt in my voice and pick up on things. She was there. And she was also a friend to my husband. She never took sides.

The pastor advised the couple to get professional help. When they started their work with a marriage counselor, Patricia said she was ready to help her husband face his problems. She did not anticipate the discovery she would make about herself. She took a hard look at her drivenness and at her tendency to set her goals unilaterally, without paying much attention to relationships. She recognized the Superwoman role she had learned from her grandmother and practiced with a vengeance: "I knew that there was so much that was demanded of me, and I wanted to do it all." Patricia was able to identify her false self and determined at once that she wanted to change. She felt that she understood Jay's side of the struggle for the first time. Central to the changes Patricia initiated in her life was her new ability to listen.

> Taking time to really be in tune with folks, to hear, and not only to hear with my ears but to use my other senses, and to make sure that I understand why I'm saying and doing what I'm saying and doing. Jay, too, learned to speak and to listen.

Patricia understood for the first time that her call directly affects her husband. With her support he was and is struggling to comprehend what it means for him to be a male spouse of a woman minister.

> When I stopped trying to fix the marriage and concentrated on fixing myself, then things began to fall back in place. When we stopped trying to focus on marriage and began to try to be the best people we could be, we discovered that we still loved each other. That was still there, but we had to find it.

In answer to the question about a time when she felt particularly good about herself, Patricia smiled a broad smile and said she felt ecstatic at her ordination. Jay was in the front row in tears when she was ordained. "That was a really important moment because he was there and it had really happened. That was a self-esteem moment."

But she wanted to speak of a second incident only two months in the past. On Christmas Eve, Patricia and Jay decided that they would have a private evening at home, without children, without friends.

> After midnight we opened gifts—and we've never done that before. . . . And on Christmas morning we went around to all the houses together and gave out the gifts. It was as if we had walked out of a chapter of a book, and turned a new leaf.

As she talked about her move from the expectations she placed on herself, many of which grew out of her admiration for her grandmother, to a new set of expectations, Patricia could see that she had come full circle. Her parents had anticipated that their only child would go through college before she would consider getting married. For years money was faithfully set aside for her schooling. She married at sixteen before finishing high school and gave birth to six children within nine years. Patricia's husband died soon after the birth of their sixth child. Several years later she remarried and returned to school. Patricia saw her return to school as "picking up the things I was supposed to do in the first place. Part of it could have been trying to fulfill expectations of wonderful child and granddaughter." (In fact, she did what Grandmother did rather than what Grandmother said. She repeated the pattern: young wife, young mother, young widow.) The turning point from another's agenda to her own came when she realized that she did not want to lose her marriage, that her relationship to Jay was centrally important to who she is and what she wants to do.

> I need to make sure about what I'm after. It makes me pull back when I get running, running, running, and stop and say: "Wait a minute, what are you doing here?" I pull back and look and ask why I am doing all this crazy stuff and really evaluate it . . . because I realize that for me, even in my commitment to God, the important thing is to always be the best person I can be. When I begin to look at the Superwoman structure, I wasn't being the best person I could be.

Paradoxically, Patricia wanted to give up Superwoman in order to be "the best" person she could be. She had been accepted at seminary and was to begin her studies midyear. She decided to take six months off and start the following fall; in the meantime she cut back on her schedule. She and Jay began a second courtship; four months later they continued their marriage, now a far more mutual and satisfying relationship.

Linda and Marian and Patricia: three women who have rewritten the ideologies that govern their lives and continue in the process of putting those ideologies into practice. The final chapter of this book explores practical ways in which women can help other women do the same. That is, it examines ways in which women can help one another transform the belief systems that govern their lives and practice those beliefs, and thus strengthen their faith in self and in God/dess and enjoy good enough self esteem.

5

Conclusion: Enacting Feminist Insights

There are still few women who can believe deeply that they are truly worthy. Likewise, the process of valuing other women has not reached full fruition.

Jean Baker Miller[1]

These disconcerting words drive home two crucial realities: women do not believe in themselves with enough conviction and passion, and women do not sufficiently value other women. In other words, faith in self as well as faith in other women is still thin; self esteem and esteem for other women remains weak. The problem resides both in how women perceive themselves and what women choose to do about those perceptions.

This book has focused primarily on understanding the dynamics of faith in self and self esteem in the lives of women: understanding how foundational self esteem grows out of early parent-child relationships; understanding that the deepest meaning of faith in oneself is of a piece with faith in God/dess who makes life holy; understanding how images of Deity influence the way a woman perceives herself; understanding the factors that shape secondary self esteem; and understanding the interrelationships among a person's self-concept, her God concept, and her ability to believe in and value herself.

Such understandings can also be expressed in terms of fundamental claims about each woman's life:

Woman was created by God/dess as man's equal: woman and man are equally worthy of respect and opportunity in all areas of human life.

Creation of human life is ongoing; under the influence of the God/dess who lives within, a woman of faith continues to shape her life day by day.

Because of the life-giving functions of a woman's body, she has awesome influence over the life of her offspring beginning at the moment of conception.

A woman whose full range of feelings is accepted by her parents from the beginning of life is able to develop her true self and enjoy good enough foundational self esteem.

The elements of a woman's secondary self esteem include the experience of respect from others, an ideology that recognizes the dignity of women, mutual relationship, competence, vocation or passion, and self-acceptance. Authentic secondary self esteem must be based on the true self.

The perpetuation of exclusively male images of Deity reinforces an incomplete and hierarchical understanding of human life and interferes with a woman's ability to experience herself as an image of God/dess.

In order for these claims to enhance a woman's faith in self and self esteem, they must be translated into behaviors; they must be enacted.

From Understanding to Enacting

This chapter shifts from understanding to *actively understanding*, that is, to enacting one's understanding of the meaning of human life and of one's place in the scheme of things. Now the focus is on practice, on actually designing ideology that supports faith in self and self esteem and on acting out of an ideology that recognizes and enhances the beauty and power of women.

It is not always easy to determine whether belief in the dignity and beauty of women comes before a woman changes her patterns of behavior or whether her patterns of behavior change before she truly believes in the dignity and beauty of women. The question of whether behavior is shaped by attitudes or attitudes follow behavior has been long debated in psychology. People who believe in insight therapy claim that once a problem is understood, the person is able to do something about it—that is, the enlightened person can change self-defeating behavior. Unless the problem is understood, habits of self-defeating behavior continue, making change more and more difficult. In other words, the *Aha!* experience or insight comes first. Behaviorists see the process in reverse. Once people change their characteristic ways of responding, behaviorists believe, their attitudes automatically change. It matters not whether the cause of the problem is understood. Act in a way conducive of self esteem, and self esteem will follow. For women who are not only trying to redesign their understanding of human life and their place in it but are also trying to put that new ideology into practice, both insight and behavioral change are necessary. Both allow a woman to gain faith in herself and to develop good enough self esteem.

Psychologists Richard L. Bednar, M. Gawain Wells, and Scott R. Peterson, authors of *Self-Esteem: Paradoxes and Innovations in Clinical Theory and Practice*, clearly vote for behavioral change as the key to high self esteem. The central conclusion they draw from years of research and clinical practice is that self esteem is achieved if a person chooses coping over avoidance when faced with conflict involving anxiety and fear. People who choose to cope with the problems they face by confronting the conflict feel good about themselves; people who deny or avoid the conflict feel bad about themselves. These three psychologists believe that assessing and altering one's level of self esteem is as simple as that. Furthermore, they point out that what results from the coping is not as important to self esteem as is the fact that the person faced the conflict rather than avoiding it. To be able to say, "I didn't succeed, but I sure gave it my best try," is what is most important. If a person initiates change in her characteristic ways of responding to unwelcome experiences, she will feel better about herself even if her attempt at a new response fails to achieve its desired effect.

A person who never confronts parents when they make excessive demands on her time, for example, may say no to a particular demand that she believes to be unreasonable. She does not want to comply to their request or demand. Her aim is to be true to herself and respect her feelings—as well as her time and energy—and at the same time sustain a connection with each of her parents. She wants to alter her relationship to them without either alienating them or cutting herself off from them. Her parents may react angrily to her unusual response and put immediate distance between themselves and their "unappreciative and disrespectful" daughter. The daughter would probably have very mixed feelings about her behavior. She might be saddened by her parents' abusive remarks as well as haunted by guilt feelings because she has made them angry. Yet, while she may feel hurt and be bothered by nagging guilt, she might at the same time be convinced that she has made the right choice. She feels better about herself for initiating a change in her lifelong pattern of being compelled to say yes to all of her parents' demands. In saying no she begins to dismantle the false self, which says she is lovable only if she is compliant and attentive to her parents' wishes, and to move toward a more honest expression of her true self. Her parents may or may not get over their disappointment that their daughter has changed the family system.

Coping is described in *Self-Esteem* as "a growth-oriented process in which personal development is the inevitable result of facing, understanding, and resolving conflict situations."[2] In the context of this book the word *confronting* is more appropriate than *coping*. Coping implies putting up with obstacles or adversity and maintaining oneself in the process. Confronting implies challenging oneself or another person or situation because a practice or expectation ought not be "put up with"—the situation cries out for change. Confronting, then, is the process through which women both rewrite the patriarchal ideology that has governed their lives and put into practice their new convictions about themselves and their place in the world.

The authors of *Self-Esteem* call the opposite of coping "avoidance": "a process we engage in that allows us to cling to our childish ideals by not facing those unpleasant psychological realities that can expose the fraud and faults in our idealistic self-conceptions."[3] In the language of this book, avoidance is a process in which a woman engages that allows her to cling to the demands of the false self and seek her self esteem through conforming to the expectations of others. When applied to women as a group, avoidance is a process women engage in that encourages them to accept their "assigned place" within a patriarchal society by not facing the painful struggle of claiming their equality to men. At least one of the reasons a woman avoids is that a majority of women avoid. Patriarchy dies hard, and a woman trying to move from avoidance to confrontation will be pressured to change back by many people around her, both men and women, who have "bought into" patriarchal roles and rules.

The concluding task of this book, then, is to understand why patriarchal ideologies remain intact, and why, when they are dismantled and replaced, rewritten ideologies are not consistently enacted. (In many cases women do enact their new ideologies and are sometimes called "man-haters" or similar derogatory terms for doing so.) The emphasis is on enacting feminist insights, doing what must be done before women can live out of new understandings of the world and their place in it.

The plan of action, which always involves insight and understanding, includes the following steps: bonding with women, confronting patriarchy, claiming the strengths of women, changing patterns of relating, and developing spiritual practices that support the true self. Finally, a step that would dramatically alter the course of history is respecting the feelings of children.

Bonding with Women

Perhaps the primary reason women have not begun to believe deeply in their own value and in that of other women is that they have not utilized their enormous ability to empower one another to break the bonds of patriarchy. Sufficient numbers of women have not yet enjoyed the remarkable experience of being empowered by another woman or by a group of women to discover and express their true selves. To be empowered by women requires special time with women. Women need to tell their stories, and they need to be heard. Otherwise they remain isolated and unknown by other women—and often trapped in patriarchal expectations. When enlightened women intentionally support other women, not only are ideologies rewritten, but behaviors change and women discover increased faith in themselves and stronger self esteem. Something happens within a group of women who have become conscious of the lack of freedom they experience in the presence of patriarchal people, men and women alike. Individually and collectively they awaken to new possibilities for themselves.

As in any group whose primary aim is mutual support, the first task is trust-building. The women must develop trust in one another and in the group before they can take the risk of self-disclosure. Then remnants of the false self can be discarded as women engage in a free exchange of experiences, feelings, ideas, and dreams. Enormous creative energy can be released and the whole gamut of emotion expressed: rage and fear and hurt, joy and humor and cheer. Through the process, women find their voices. The more introverted women's voices often have been inhibited and suppressed; for such women, finding their voices can be both a terrifying and an ecstatic experience. Nelle Morton's well-known quotation best describes the power of women's bonding: Women "hear one another into speech."[4] In the hearing and in the speaking they not only come to faith in themselves and in other women, they also delight in their discovery of one another. The group itself takes on a unique existence. Both intentionally and unconsciously, bonded women redesign their understanding of the world and their place in it and find the motivation and courage to enact their insights.

Within patriarchal society, women have been educated to believe that a woman's central task in life is winning a male partner—the "prize" who will be protector, provider, and father of her children. During their youth many women often compete for the better prizes. They learn to see one another as threats as they subtly or blatantly compete for the prizes. In women's groups, women come to appreciate themselves and one another as the first prize.[5] Only when a woman has come to believe in herself and in other women is she truly ready to share life with an equal partner—male or female. Only when a single woman has come to believe in herself and in other women is she truly ready to accept the fact that she can live a full life without a primary partner. Reframing women's singleness is one of the many chores of confronting patriarchy, the next task in enacting feminist insights.

Confronting Patriarchy

Patriarchy dies hard because the vast majority of men and a perhaps critical mass of women are still blind to the domination/subordination soul of patriarchy. Fantasies replace facts in the imaginations of so many people.

For example, many people still repeat the cliché that it's not the men who rule the world but the powerful woman behind each ruling man.

A neighbor recently asked about my work on this book. When I told him that I was "rediscovering woman in patriarchal society," he suggested I had things in reverse. "We live in a matriarchy. It's really the women who have the power." This distorted thinking is based on the fact that many women overfunction in the home and as a consequence have a controlling influence on the emotional lives of their children and sometimes of their spouses.

Only a small percentage of heterosexual men choose to live without a woman, and most women overfunction both for their children and for their partners. Women generally carry primary responsibility for the physical and emotional needs of the family. On a day-to-day basis, mothers have more influence than fathers over the lives of their children. This influence may continue within the extended family as grandmothers involve themselves in the lives of their adult children and grandchildren. Unless the patriarchal ideology that keeps women powerful within the home and largely invisible in the public arena is understood, the conclusion that "women have the power" can cloud the truth that men are in control of most political, economic, medical, and educational structures around the world. Women must insist on shared responsibility within the home and increase their visibility in the public arena in order truly to confront patriarchy.

The wives of men who have climbed to prominence have been educated to take major or even total responsibility for the home and children and at the same time center their lives on their husbands' careers. Most often this means forgoing their own career interests or educational pursuits. They study *his* world and gain wisdom that makes the couple codependent or irreplaceable partners. Each needs the other in order to maintain her or his identity. However, the same dynamic does not often show up when women become the political leaders and professionals. In those cases, men run on a parallel track, pursuing their educations and developing their careers. There are few women in top executive positions, and no one expects the husbands of these women to shape their lives around their wives' careers. While the wife of the company president could both provide emotional support and interest in her husband's world and at the same time discover and develop her own creative potential, many wives of professional men fail to pursue such a course. (Of course, men, too, can both develop their potential and provide emotional support and interest in their wives' worlds.)

Another reason for the skewed notion that "we live in a matriarchy" is that many men have been dominated by the mothers whom patriarchy sets up to overfunction in their lives. In other words, women have dominated in the home because men have played a lesser role in the everyday lives of their children. Men overfunction in the work world and underfunction in the home. Women overfunction in the home and underfunction in the work world. Consequently many men do not know how to relate to the few women who have made their way into the ruling structures of male institutions except as dominating mother figures.

The bottom line is that many women have a very difficult time enacting a belief in their intrinsic worth as men's equals. Consciously or unconsciously, too many women continue to assume that the man's career comes first. Patriarchy has successfully educated women into a second-class citizenship that leaves them driven to prove their (false-self) worth—and generally that entails finding acceptance in the eyes of men. Only when they genuinely value their true selves as women and discover the intrinsic worth of other women will they be able to break the bonds of patriarchy, which makes recognition by men all-essential to women. If a critical mass of women is able to break the bonds of patriarchy, the women who live in a post-patriarchal world will know their intrinsic worth and the value of other women long before they seek the mutual acceptance and love of men. Some will know their emotional and sexual satisfaction in a mutual relationship with a woman. Others will remain single.

In patriarchal society single women are often seen as odd, lonely, pathetic people who have somehow missed the boat. Sharon Hicks and Carol Anderson claim that our society sees singles in general as "selfish, irresponsible, hedonistic, immature, possible victims of pathological personality development, even 'schizoid'." The never-married woman is seen as "a pathetic, tragic figure who clearly cannot be happy without the joys of a husband and children."[6] They suggest that therapists working with single or childless women refrain from offering empathy for their lonely existence and instead point to the negative mental health implications attached to marriage and motherhood in our society.[7] Studies support the view that social role plays a part in the vulnerability of women to depression. Whereas marriage protects men from depression, it is detrimental to women.[8] Some separated or divorcing women are sometimes surprised to discover a great sense of relief and freedom when their dissatisfying marriages are finally over, even when they struggled to the end to keep their marriages intact.

Women must stop avoiding the anxiety and fear that confronting patriarchy inevitably entails. They have to engage in both individual and collective confrontation in order to arrive at faith in their true selves and good enough self esteem. The self-confrontation is most effectively done within relationships to other women. Women therapists, teachers, and ministers express great excitement and sometimes awe in speaking of the challenge and satisfaction they experience when they are able to empower a woman to confront the injustice and abuse she has lived with in her marriage or workplace or family of origin. The same satisfaction is experienced when women friends are able to empower one another to break the bonds of patriarchy. Some women have been surprised by the insights and lifestyles of adolescent and young adult daughters, which trigger enormous creative changes in the lives of their mothers. The exciting fact is that women empower and support and sustain women. In the public sector, groups of women have worked on committees and task forces to publicize the abuse of women in institutions, whether it be unequal pay scales and benefits, hiring and promotion procedures, or sexual/gender abuse within the organization. Some women who choose to stay in institutional churches seek ways to make both church structure and formal worship more just and inclusive. Other women put their energy into Women-Church, where the beauty and dignity of women is a foundational belief. Confronting patriarchy either in oneself or another, in one's private or public life, requires the support of other women. Miriam Greenspan's words are a call to the task of mutual commitment to confrontation: "The power of self-esteem women long for cannot be separated from the power for women that comes from fighting for ourselves and each other."[9]

Claiming the Strengths of Women

Becoming a true self demands that women break the habit of conforming to patriarchal notions of who women should be: docile, subordinate, dependent, overfunctioners in the home, underfunctioners in "the world." To conform to such a false female self promoted by patriarchy is to conform to low self esteem. Women must also claim with genuine pride the values society has typically assigned to women as second-class values: nurture, care, responsibility, empathy, cooperativeness, mutual relations. Women have the capacity to bring those precious values into whatever arena they enter. Males typically value individuation and achievement over women's more prized values of responsibility and relationship. Feminist theorists have challenged male models of human and ethical development that assume that autonomy and individual rights reflect greater maturity than care and attachment.[10] Confrontation of those models must spread through all aspects of social life: government, business, education, medicine, law, religion. A far greater number of women leaders deserve a chance as chief executive officers, university presidents, newspaper editors, congresspersons, and governors; women deserve a chance in the White House and in representing the United States at summit meetings. Women will surely not establish a matriarchy, and no one yet knows what face society might wear under women's leadership, but certainly nurture, care, responsibility, empathy, cooperativeness, and mutual relations would be esteemed values in such a society.

Changing Patterns of Relating

For many women the process of coming to self-acceptance requires that old patterns of relationship be broken: patterns of relationship with oneself, with family and friends, and with God/dess. When a woman has lived a major part of her life according to others' expectations, her false self has become something of a permanent partner who automatically takes over and performs according to years of rehearsal. The false self has memorized the lines to perfection and knows all of the gestures and stage directions written into the script.

What I have learned about my own well-practiced performance is that a particular kind of occasion generally intimidates me—situations in which a sizable group of men and a minority of women share intellectual ideas, or in which I make myself vulnerable within such a group of colleagues by offering an intellectual idea that is still in process. (Similarly, I can be intimidated by an intellectual woman if I allow my competitive false self to be in control.) A typical false-self reaction to the intimidation is a rush of self-doubt. Are my convictions sound? Is this idea worth exploring? Will I be found illogical or inarticulate or overemotional? Will I cry? Recently I felt intimidated by one of my "authorities" and reacted out of an old tape. "I've been fooling myself. My logic is weak." To my delight a voice within, which I gladly ascribe to the God/dess who has made her home in me, drowned out the negative thinking with this message: "Don't you dare give your power away."

It is precisely at such moments that I know God/dess as Goddess. I knew without doubt that the power she spoke of was the power of my true self. Empowered by that surge of faith and confidence, I spoke out of my owned authority and so enacted my life-enhancing ideology. Each such enactment strengthens the true self and weakens the lingering claims of patriarchy. Since that wonderful experience I have said to myself in advance of potentially intimidating occasions, "Don't you dare give your power away." Old behavioral reactions of the false self can indeed be replaced by confident responses of the true self as women discover themselves in patriarchal society and work toward the conversion of that society.

Women who have discovered their true selves relate to men as their equals and expect men to do the same. For many women this requires a new set of behavioral responses to spouses, co-workers, people in authority positions, even to strangers on the street and in the marketplace. Sometimes this means reminding people that their language excludes women. Sometimes this requires renegotiating responsibilities so that women are not the assumed providers of physical needs but co-providers with their male partners and co-workers. Sometimes this entails organized responses to institutional inequities, whether it be equal pay for equal work or equal access to the more attractive and creative job responsibilities. Sometimes this includes writing and enacting grievance procedures, or revising bylaws and mission statements and any other patriarchal documents that govern institutions until women are truly respected as men's equals.

Women must also break the covenant between their false self and a false God.[11] The Deity who creates and loves the world is not the Ultimate Patriarch who has a design on every aspect of a person's life (which gets translated by lesser patriarchs as the "will of God"). Nor does the Deity seek obedient children who relate to the Holy One as to a parent who knows best what "his" children should do. Rather, God/dess seeks ongoing, vital incarnate relationships with thinking, feeling, choosing, passionate people who, under the inspiration of the Spirit within, co-create their lives day by day. To enact one's belief that religion is essentially a vital relationship with the Holy One is to live a profoundly creative spiritual life. This kind of spiritual relationship results in a continuation of the struggle for equality and justice and love that set the agenda in Jesus' life. Like Jesus, women inspired by the Holy One confront themselves and other people and institutions day by day, repeatedly asking how best to respond to the challenges of life. The question in a given situation is not so much, "Where is God's will?" Rather, the question becomes, "God/dess, what do we do with this one?" Women need continually to rethink and rework their understanding of God's will and God's presence in their lives. Women are not only children of God; they are co-creators with the God/dess of their own lives and of their communities.

Developing Spiritual Practices that Support the True Self

Many women have found empowering spiritual practices that either replace the practices they developed within patriarchal religion or simply express them in more inclusive form. Several possibilities are offered here.[12]

The first is for a woman to discover and be with the Goddess who is with her. To discover the Goddess is to know the one we call God in a more inclusive way, in a way that helps a woman know herself as holy. To discover the Goddess, then, is to discover the one God/dess. A woman cannot come close to Goddess in prayer without coming closer to herself, the self as known by God/dess. To turn to God/dess in prayer, especially in the midst of personal turmoil, is to find perspective. Immediate concerns, as much as they matter to the Holy One, matter not so much because of the importance of the particular issue but because these concerns have an impact on the way a woman is present to herself, to others, and therefore to God/dess.

Some women find it helpful to use a familiar set of respected words in times of silent prayer, and when conflict stirs up self-doubt in their everyday life, they return to their chosen word or words for an immediate faith perspective. These words may be God images or symbols from childhood; favorite scriptural images of Deity; words that one has reflected upon and come to cherish: "Holy One," "Sophia Wisdom," "Oh, Goddess," "Be still my soul," "This is my body."

A student once told this memorable story in the context of a classroom discussion about images of God. An elderly woman friend of her family was accustomed to driving herself to night meetings, much to the concern of her friends. On one late-evening occasion, when she walked to the parking lot to get into her car, she noticed that the small front window or vent on the passenger side had been removed. Frightened, she hurried into the driver's seat to make a quick escape. A man's arm came through the opening. He unlocked the door, got into the car, and told her to drive away and do exactly as he said. Terrified, she held tight to the steering wheel and screamed, "I am covered with feathers, I am covered with feathers, I am covered with feathers." Her frightened assailant jumped out of the car and fled. "Feathers" had long been one of her favorite metaphors of God. She had often prayed the passage from Psalm 91:4, "[God] covers you with [God's] feathers, and you find shelter underneath [God's] wings."

Another path toward increased faith in self, faith in God/dess, and good enough self esteem is related to the use of cherished words that have been both personalized and empowered through prayer. Reflective reading of inspiring material often helps women discover themselves. The Christian tradition has called the prayerful reading

of scripture *lectio divina*. Words that reveal the heart of
God/dess are savored in silent meditation.

> No need to recall the past,
> no need to think about what was done before.
> See, I am doing a new deed,
> even now it comes to light; can you not see it?
> (Isa. 43:18–19a)

Now [God] is the Spirit, and where the Spirit of [God] is,
there is freedom. And we, with our unveiled faces reflecting
like mirrors the brightness of [God], all grow brighter and
brighter as we are turned into the image that we reflect; this
is the work of [God] who is Spirit.

(2 Cor. 3:18)

Lectio divina results in scriptural passages becoming
truly one's own. Revered words become part of one's
psyche and an ordinary response to life. "Where the
Spirit of God is, there is freedom" invites a woman to
discover both Spirit of God and freedom as she makes
day-by-day decisions about her life.

Any reading material that a woman finds inspiring,
life-giving, or mind- and heart-opening can be used as
her *lectio divina*—words of faith or hope or love that
bring her closer to the true self and therefore to the true
God/dess. An increasing number of women are publish-
ing articles and books about women's spirituality that
deserve prayerful, reflective reading as well as serious
study.[13]

Still another way to become more aware of the influence of the Holy One is to take time to process one's
reactions to everyday events in light of a woman's faith
in herself and her faith in the presence of God/dess. If
a person becomes aware of negative feelings or dissatisfying responses to unwelcome experiences, she can
develop the habit of a "faith pause." A faith pause is a
pregnant moment in which one tries to discern spiritually
what is happening within one's mind and heart in order
to respond as creatively as possible to everyday events.
For example, if a woman is aware of either being treated
with disrespect or of being disrespectful toward herself,

she takes time to prayerfully reflect on her thoughts and feelings. If God/dess is invited to share in the reflection, to enlighten her understanding of what is going on, the most creative possibility for that moment in time becomes clearer. Thinking through what is happening inside may include describing the negative cycles of thought and feeling or the specific blockage to oneself and then asking how faith in the Holy Presence informs these thoughts and feelings. A positive response to the situation amounts to co-creating with God/dess the next moment of one's life, and in the process increasing faith in self and self esteem. (It was in a faith pause that I heard the strong directive: "Don't you dare give your power away.") At times it is useful to share one's resolve with a trusted friend. This makes good intentions more public and, as a result, more specific and more firmly held. When a woman of faith shares her resolve with a friend, she has made herself accountable to God/dess, to herself, and to her friend.

Respecting the Feelings of Children

Finally, an obvious way to act on the understandings included in this book is to change both attitudes and behaviors toward children that in any way demean them or keep them from developing their true selves. If little girls were raised out of a new appreciation for the beauty of women, and with deeper respect for their own feelings and thoughts, they would have few problems with weak faith in themselves that comes out of low foundational self esteem. A parallel claim could easily be made about the parenting of boys. Perhaps the words of Alice Miller ought to be posted on every nursery door: "If a mother respects both herself and her child from [the] very first day onward, she will never need to teach [her child] respect for others."[14] In an ideal world, respect would be the ordinary gift one gives to children. Miller's directive to mothers belongs to fathers, siblings, grandparents and godparents, relatives, teachers, baby-sitters, friends and acquaintances, even strangers who pass children in the grocery store. If everyone respected themselves and all children, children would respect themselves and others.

In addition to meeting their physical needs, respect for children involves intentional presence to them: acknowledging all of their feelings, hearing their thoughts, witnessing the demonstration of their new skills, encouraging their ability to make choices, sharing in their discovery of nature and of themselves. Since women still carry most of the responsibility for children, their power to encourage the development of the true self that knows good enough self esteem is awesome. But before women can provide children with such empowering respect, they must respect themselves and other women.

At the opening of this chapter it was suggested that the problem women have in believing deeply that they are worthy and in valuing other women resides both in how women perceive themselves and what women choose to do about those perceptions. Women need other women in order to solve the problem. They need expansive ideologies that recognize at every level of human life that women are images of the Holy One and that women are men's equals. They need the support of women and of understanding men to put into practice what they believe about their dignity and power. Bonded with women who have rediscovered their beauty and holiness, strengthened by their faith in the magnificence of life, women are then prepared to behold the "new thing" springing forth within themselves. The "new thing" is holy woman, the image of God/dess and the home of the God/dess. Living out a new ideology that truly proclaims in word and expresses in action their creative gifts, women are able to name their values, discover their passion, and build competence and confidence in themselves. They have faith in themselves. They have faith in God/dess. And they enjoy good enough self esteem. Together they can not only discover themselves and one another in patriarchal society, but they can look forward to the day when patriarchy will be a thing of the past.

Now [God] is the Spirit, and where the Spirit of [God] is, there is freedom. And we, with our unveiled faces reflecting like mirrors the brightness of [God], all grow brighter and brighter as we are turned into the image that we reflect; this is the work of [God] who is Spirit.

(2 Cor. 3:18)

No need to recall the past,
no need to think about what was done before.
See, I am doing a new deed,
even now it comes to light; can you not see it?
(Isa. 43:18–19a)

A True Self/ True Goddess Moment to Remember

Goddess Grace
I breathe your singing Spring
with sweet heartache
    bubbling joy and
    rush of ecstasy
    a pounding, bursting ache.

        Be.
        Just be.
        And let the warm caress of possibility
        Of **Yes**
            connecting
            reaching out and in
        Just let it be.
        Let yourself be splashing gratitude.

Spirit Goddess
Holy inspiration
Woman's recreation

Bless
Bless
Yes.

                        Carroll Saussy

Appendix A
Results of the Faith and Self-Esteem Inventory Questionnaire

The questionnaire was distributed to 405 persons in a seminary community; 145 were returned. Data about the respondents follows:

Sex: M: 62 (43%) F: 83 (57%)

Age: under 30: 26 (18%); 30–39: 43 (30%); 40–49: 45 (31%); 50–59: 26 (18%); over 60: 4 (3%) [note 61% between 30 and 49]. One person did not indicate age.

Religious affiliation: United Methodists: 88 (61%); Presbyterian Church (USA): 11 (8%); Unitarian Universalist: 9 (6%); Episcopal: 7 (5%); United Church of Christ: 4 (3%); Baptist: 4 (3%); below 3%: Roman Catholic: 3; Christian: 3; Lutheran: 2; Christian Methodist Episcopal: 1; Metropolitan Community Church: 1; Seventh Day Adventist: 1; "ecumenical": 1; African Methodist Episcopal: 1; Universal: 1; Reformed Latter Day Saints: 1; Protestant: 2; none listed: 5.

Occupation: minister (pastor, clergy, chaplain): 42 (29%); student: 30 (21%); professor (teacher, educator): 18 (12%); administrator: 12 (8%); administrative assistant: 3; seminary staff: 3; counselor: 2; musician: 2; nurse: 2; scientist: 2; director of religious education: 2; 1 each of the following: accountant, attorney, consultant, construction estimator, development coordinator, developmental aid for mentally retarded, economist, electrical engineer, federal government, finance, insurance agent, mechanic, media, policy analyst, retired, secretary, social worker, tax preparer, writer; no occupation listed: 8.

Highest academic degree: doctorate: 22; master's: 41; bachelor's: 69; JD: 3; LLB: 1; Dip. Theo: 1; associate's: 1; high school: 3; none listed: 4.

1. How would you rate the level of self esteem in your present life (self esteem understood as a generally positive self-evaluation)?

		Total	Male	Female
A.	consistently high	46 (32%)	29 (47%)	18 (22%)
B.	more frequently high than low	65 (45%)	18 (29%)	46 (55%)
C.	as often high as low	25 (17%)	13 (21%)	12 (14%)
D.	more frequently low than high	7 (5%)	1	6 (7%)
E.	consistently low	1	0	1
F.	No answer	1		

2. Do you consider self esteem to be a problem with which you currently struggle?

Total	Male	Female
Yes 53 (36.5%)	18 (29%)	35 (42%)
No 89 (61%)	43 (69%)	46 (55%)

sometimes—1   no response—2

3. Rate yourself with regard to the following components of self esteem: 1 = low (lacking in that quality) to 5 = high (strong in the area). (Note: total response does not equal 145 in most cases because some items on the scale were not checked.)

			1	2	3	4	5
A.	I have a solid sense of who I am and what I value.		0	1	13	58	72
		% =				40	50
B.	I have a realistic assessment of my gifts and talents.		1	7	21	74	40
		% =				51	28

C. I experience the affection and approval of my parents and/or other significant members of my family of origin.

		10	14	22	32	66
% =					22	46

D. I experience the affection and approval of members of my adult family.

		3	11	18	40	73
% =					28	50

E. I feel significant to important people in my life.

		1	10	20	42	70
% =					29	48

F. I sense that others view me in relatively the same way that I perceive myself.

		6	20	33	64	22
% =				23	44	15

G. I feel close to significant people in my life.

		2	4	16	55	64
% =					38	44

H. I have a sense of separateness or being able to stand on my own.

		2	4	17	60	61
% =					41	42

I. I experience myself as a competent person.

		1	3	11	74	56
% =					51	39

J. I am able to live up to my beliefs and values.

		0	7	31	67	33
% =				21	46	23

K. I am able to handle negative experience reasonably well.

		2	14	35	70	21
% =				24	48	14

Are there other specific factors or particular experiences which you believe enhance your self esteem? Comment:

(1) 42 (29%) comments related to success or achievement
(2) 22 (15%) commented on God/Christ's love
(3) 13 (9%) mentioned relationships outside family
(4) 5 (3%) mentioned positive family relationships

Are there other specific factors or particular experiences which you believe weaken your self esteem? Comment:

(1) 57 (39%) made comments related to personal inadequacies or failures, or negative social experiences

(2) 18 (12%) mentioned negative relationships within family of origin

(3) 5 (3%), separation or divorce

4. Have there been times in your life when self esteem stood out as a significant problem?

Yes   120 (83%)   No   22 (15%)   No answer   3

If yes, was this (check any periods that apply) during child-hood   40 (28%), adolescence   88 (61%), young adult-hood   62 (43%), middle adulthood   19 (13%).

Comment:

(1) 38 (26%) mentioned personal inadequacies or failure or negative social experience

(2) 13 (9%) commented on negative experiences in family of origin

(3) 12 (8%), divorce or marital problems

(4) 4 specified problems women face in patriarchal society

5. Have there been times in your life when your self esteem was notably high?

Yes   115 (79%)   No   23 (16%)   No answer   7 (5%)

If yes, was this during childhood   19 (13%), adoles-cence   19 (13%), young adulthood   49 (34%), middle adulthood   66 (45.5%). (Note: Some respondents indicated more than one period in which self esteem was notably high.)

Comment: A vast majority of the answers related experi-ences of success and recognition; a small number speci-fied religious calling and positive experiences of parenting.

6. Would you describe yourself as a religious or spiritual person, i.e., a person who has developed a God-focused worldview that influences your daily life?

Yes   135 (93%)   No   6 (4%)   No answer   4

If yes: When your self esteem is at risk, does your religious faith help you maintain a positive attitude about yourself?

Yes 126 (87%) No 8 (5.5%) Sometimes 1 Maybe 1

Comment: Fifty-one (35%) specified that prayer, meditation, and faith in God's presence and love enhanced their sense of self or self esteem. A small number of persons explained that they do not use faith to support their self esteem or do not relate religion and self esteem.

7. *Was religious faith an important part of your childhood and adolescence?*

Yes 107 (74%) No 21 (14%) Both 11 (8%)

Maybe 3 No answer 3

If yes, do you think that your religious beliefs helped or hindered your self esteem? (Note: Some respondents who had not checked "yes" answered this question.)

Helped 100 (69%) Hindered 8 (5.5%) Both 19 (13%)

Comment: Nineteen respondents (13%) mentioned the negative influence of a punishing or hierarchical God/religion. Positive comments related mainly to the importance of church experience to one's sense of identity and meaning.

8. *Do you participate in structured religious disciplines such as prayer, contemplative reading, meditation, community worship, or work for social justice?*

Yes 135 (93%) No 8 (5.5%) Sometimes 1 No answer 1

If yes, do you experience a relationship between your religious practices and your self esteem?

Yes 123 (85%) No 5 (3%) Maybe 1

? 1 Both 3 No answer 2

Comment: While most comments affirmed a relationship between religious practice and self esteem, one person wrote a strong statement against the word "discipline" as dichotomizing and lacking spontaneity.

9. Which of the two would you say is more accurate:
A. Self esteem is something that we work to achieve through attending to circumstances that build or reduce our positive self-feelings and making changes in our negative thinking and/or behavior.

116 (80%)

B. Self esteem is something that takes us by surprise; we don't need to consciously work on increasing self esteem.

14 (10%)   Both   8 (5.5%)   Neither   3

False dichotomy   1   No answer   3

10. Please make any additional comments about self esteem and/or faith and self esteem.
Comments that did not duplicate those already mentioned included questions about early Christian mystics' low self esteem as an ideal, the need to take responsibility for self and not rely on pleasing others, the difficulty for women ever to feel consistently good about themselves in a patriarchal society.

Appendix B
Commentary on the Results of the Faith and Self-Esteem Inventory Questionnaire

The first time it was used, the inventory was sent to a total of 405 persons in a seminary community—205 women and 200 men. Returns came from 42% of the women and 32.5% of the men. Of the 151 returns, 145 were received in time to be included in these results. (The following comments are based only on the first use of the Self-Esteem Inventory. A revised version of the inventory, Appendix C, has since been used in a variety of settings.)

Respondents were asked to rate the level of self esteem in their present lives on a five-point scale (consistently high, more frequently high than low, as often high as low, more frequently low than high, consistently low). Thirty-two percent marked "consistently high," 45% "more frequently high than low." "As often high as low" was the answer on 17% of the responses. Only 5% marked "more frequently low than high," and less than 1% chose the lowest point on the scale.

In response to the second question, asking if self esteem is a current problem, 61% answered "no"; 36.5%, "yes."

There were gender-related differences in response to the above questions:

1. Forty-seven percent of the men but only 22% of the women answered that they had consistently high self es-

teem. Twenty-nine percent of the men answered "more frequently high than low," while 55% of the women chose that response.

2. The difference between men and women choosing a combination of consistently high and more frequently high was slight: 76% men, 77% women. However, while fewer than 1% of the men said they had more frequently low or consistently low self esteem, more than 7% of the women rated themselves in the lowest two categories.

3. Forty-two percent of the women compared to 29% of the men consider self esteem to be a problem with which they currently struggle.

The third item asked respondents to rate themselves on a five-point scale, from weak (1) to strong (5), for each of eleven components of self esteem. More than 90% of the respondents circled 4 or 5 on statements A and I: "I have a solid sense of who I am and what I value," and "I experience myself as a competent person." More than 80% claimed the same strength in responding to G and H: "I feel close to significant people in my life," and "I have a sense of separateness or being able to stand on my own"; more than 70% in response to B, D, and E: "I have a realistic assessment of my gifts and talents"; "I experience the affection and approval of members of my adult family"; "I feel significant to important people in my life." More than 60% circled 4 or 5 in response to items C, F, J, and K: "I experience the affection and approval of my parents and/or other significant members of my family of origin"; "I sense that others view me in relatively the same way that I perceive myself"; "I am able to live up to my beliefs and values"; and "I am able to handle negative experience reasonably well." While only slightly more than one-third of the respondents consider self esteem to be a current problem, 83% say that self esteem stood out as a significant problem at some point in their lives. Sixty-one percent of the total checked adolescence as a time when they struggled with self esteem (while 13% said that adolescence was a time when their self esteem was notably high); 43% struggled with self esteem during young adulthood; 28% during childhood and 13% during middle adulthood.

While not all respondents have reached it, middle adulthood stood out as the greatest period of high self esteem, 45.5% of the total group; followed by young adulthood, 34%; childhood and adolescence each were times of high self esteem for 13% of the respondents.

In answer to both question 6, whether the person considered her/himself to be a religious or spiritual person, and question 8, whether the person participates in structured religious practices, 93% of the total group answered "yes." Of those 135 persons, 93% (87% of the total) believe that religious faith helps maintain a positive attitude about self.

Religious faith was an important part of the childhood and adolescence of 74% of the respondents; for almost all of them religious beliefs helped their self esteem. Eighty-five percent of the total group experiences a relationship between religious practice and self esteem.

The ninth question asked respondents to choose between two statements, one suggesting that self esteem is something we work to achieve, the other that self esteem is a gift that takes us by surprise. Eighty percent said we work to achieve self esteem; 10% believe that it takes us by surprise. The choice was problematic for twelve individuals, who either said that both statements are true, or simply could not answer.

There were eight places on the inventory where the respondent could make comments, including the last item, which asked for a general comment about faith and self esteem. (Nine women and thirteen men made no comments.) Several patterns emerged in these comments:

1. When asked if factors others than those listed as components of self esteem enhance the self esteem of the respondent, the largest number of comments (approximately 42 or 29% of the whole) were related to experiences of success or achievement. Similarly, the largest number of comments regarding factors or experiences that weaken self esteem were related to failure, negative

social experience, or feelings of personal inadequacy (approximately 57 or 39% of the sample).

2. Comments about God or Christ's love as enhancing self esteem appeared on 22 or 15% of the responses. Comments throughout the inventory stressed a belief that religious faith and spiritual practices enhance or help one sustain self esteem.

3. More women than men underscored that separation and/or divorce had a devastating effect on self esteem.

4. More women than men wrote of successful parenting as contributing to positive self esteem.

5. While eighteen comments made by women indicated that patriarchy—in the home and/or in the church—weakened self esteem, *no men spoke explicitly of gender-related problems.* Women's comments about sexism include: patriarchy in the church, including exclusively male God images and a narrow view of women (8); second-class citizenship in family and society (5); sexual or physical assault within the home (2); the negative effects of being in a full-time role as housewife and mother (2). Some specific comments regarding sexism:

> Do women in patriarchy ever feel really consistently good about themselves or are we always battling the demons of second-class citizenship?

> Secular psychologies that advocate coping undermine self esteem for women and people of color.

> Particularly for women it is essential to know who you are, what your aims are, and how you can accomplish them.

Reflection on the results of the inventories led to the conviction that a pencil-and-paper research instrument needed to be replaced by in-depth conversations with women in order to better understand the gap between faith in a loving God/dess and their faith in themselves.

Appendix C
Faith and Self-Esteem Inventory Questionnaire

Note: The questionnaire in Appendix C includes revisions of the one tabulated in Appendix A.

First, in question 1 "consistently high" was replaced by "high" since there is no such thing as consistently high self esteem. "Consistently low" was replaced by "low" for the same reason.

Several changes have been made to clarify and reduce repetition in item 3:

1. To the statement in letter "C" I have changed "significant members of my family of origin" to "significant family members" and added "if not, I am able to cope with their disapproval or rejection."

2. "I experience the affection and approval of members of my adult family" (D) was deleted.

3. The words "and close" were added in the statement: "I feel significant and close to important people in my life."

4. The words "people important to me" replaced "others" in the statement: "I sense that people important to me view me in relatively the same way that I perceive myself."

5. "I feel close to significant people in my life" was deleted; the point was covered in the revised item "D".

6. "I have a sense of separateness or being able to stand on my own" became "I am able to take a stand and pursue my goals without yielding to pressures to conform to goals set for me by others."

7. "I have mutually supportive relationships within a group of peers or colleagues" was added.

The words "believes in a transcendent reality which influences" replaced "has developed a God-focused worldview that influences" in question 6.

Question 7, "Was religious faith an important part of your childhood and adolescence?", was deleted because the answer to this question came up under other items.

Question 8 was added: "Would you say that you have achieved a strong *faith in yourself*, i.e., that you view yourself as a person of intrinsic value and beauty, a person able to develop your potential? If no, what do you see as a major obstacle to your having faith in yourself?"

Finally, the words "attending to circumstances that build or reduce our positive self-feelings and" were dropped and "consciously" was added before "making changes" in question 9A. The order of the words "consciously work" in 9B was reversed.

The request for comments after all items except questions 8 and 10 was eliminated.

Faith and Self-Esteem Inventory

Data about the respondent:

Sex   M_____ F_____
Age   under 30_____   30–39_____   40–49_____
　　　50–59_____   over 60_____
Religious affiliation_____
Occupation _____ Highest academic degree _____

1. How would you rate the level of self esteem in your present life (self esteem to be understood as a generally positive self-evaluation)?

    A.　high　　　　　　　　　　　　　　　　_____
    B.　more frequently high than low　　　_____
    C.　as often high as low　　　　　　　　_____
    D.　more frequently low than high　　　_____
    E.　low　　　　　　　　　　　　　　　　_____

2. Do you consider self esteem to be a problem with which you currently struggle?

             Yes _____   No _____

3. Rate yourself with regard to the following components of self esteem: 1 = low (lacking in that quality) to 5 = high (strong in that area).

    A.　I have a solid sense of who I am and　　1 2 3 4 5
       what I value.
    B.　I have a realistic assessment of my gifts　1 2 3 4 5
       and talents.
    C.　I experience the affection and approval　1 2 3 4 5
       of my parents and/or other significant
       family members; if not, I am able to
       cope with their disapproval or
       rejection.
    D.　I feel significant and close to important　1 2 3 4 5
       people in my life.
    E.　I experience myself as a competent　　1 2 3 4 5
       person.
    F.　I sense that people important to me　　1 2 3 4 5
       view me in relatively the same way
       that I perceive myself.

G. I am able to take a stand and pursue   1 2 3 4 5
   my goals without yielding to pressures
   to conform to goals set for me by
   others.

H. I have mutually supportive   1 2 3 4 5
   relationships within a group of peers or
   colleagues.

I. I am able to live up to my beliefs and   1 2 3 4 5
   values.

J. I am able to handle negative experience   1 2 3 4 5
   reasonably well.

4. Have there been times in your life when self esteem stood out as a significant problem?

Yes _____   No _____

If yes, was this (check any periods that apply) during childhood _____, adolescence _____, young adulthood _____, middle adulthood _____.

5. Have there been times in your life when your self esteem was notably high?

Yes _____   No _____

If yes, was this during childhood _____, adolescence _____, young adulthood _____, middle adulthood _____.

6. Would you describe yourself as a religious or spiritual person, i.e., a person who believes in a transcendent reality which influences daily life?

Yes _____   No _____

If yes, when your self esteem is at risk, does religious faith help you maintain a positive attitude about yourself?

Yes _____   No _____

7. Do you participate in structured religious disciplines such as prayer, contemplative reading, meditation, community worship, or work for social justice?

Yes _____   No _____

If yes, do you experience a relationship between your religious practices and your self esteem?

Yes _____   No _____

8. Would you say that you have achieved a strong *faith in yourself*, i.e., that you view yourself as a person of intrinsic value and beauty, a person able to develop your potential?

Yes _____   No _____

If no, what do you see as a major obstacle to your having faith in yourself? Comment:

9. Which of the two would you say is more accurate:

_____A. Self esteem is something that we work to achieve through consciously making changes in our negative thinking and/or behavior.

_____ B. Self esteem is something that takes us by surprise; we don't need to work consciously on increasing self esteem.

10. On the back of the page, please make additional comments about self esteem and/or faith and self esteem.

Notes

Introduction

1. Rita Nakashima Brock, *Journeys by Heart: A Christology of Erotic Power* (New York: Crossroad, 1988), p. 7.

2. *Baedeker's Greece*, (Englewood Cliffs, N.J.: Prentice-Hall, n.d.), pp. 123–124.

3. The term *good enough self esteem* is based on D. W. Winnicott's expression "good enough mothering," a concept used to describe adequate parenting that allows the child to arrive at a realistic sense of self. See *The Maturational Processes and the Facilitating Environment: Studies in the Theory of Emotional Development* (London: Hogarth Press, 1965 copyright, 1982, fifth impression), p. 145. Good enough mothering will be discussed in chapter 1. For a concise explanation of "good enough mothering" see the chapter on Winnicott in Michael St. Clair, *Object Relations and Self Psychology: An Introduction* (Monterey, Calif.: Brooks/Cole, 1986), pp. 70–71.

4. This was the initial question Michael R. Jackson asked his interviewees in an important self-esteem project, which resulted in the book *Self-Esteem and Meaning: A Life Historical Investigation* (Albany, N.Y.: State University of New York Press, 1984). Jackson's work will be discussed in chapter 3.

5. Richard L. Bednar, M. Gawain Wells, Scott R. Peterson, *Self-Esteem: Paradoxes and Innovations in Clinical Theory and Practice* (Washington, D.C.: American Psychological Association, 1989), p. 118.

Chapter 1

1. John McDargh, *Psychoanalytic Object Relations Theory and the Study of Religion: On Faith and the Imaging of God* (Lanham, Md.: University Press of America, 1983), p. 215.

2. Several of the concepts of the British object relations theorists are used in this book, especially those of Donald Winnicott, and of the German theorist Alice Miller. However the word *object*, which in object relations theory denotes the introjected perceptions of mother/other and self, is replaced by the word *memory*.

3. D. W. Winnicott, *Playing and Reality* (New York: Basic Books, 1971), p. 112.

4. Rita Nakashima Brock, "And a Little Child Will Lead Us: Christology and Child Abuse," in *Christianity, Patriarchy, And Abuse: A Feminist Critique*, Joanne Carlson Brown and Carole R. Bohn, eds. (New York: Pilgrim Press, 1989), p.50.

5. Alice Miller, *The Drama of the Gifted Child* (New York: Basic Books, 1981), p. 32.

6. Ibid., p. 12.

7. Winnicott, *Maturational Processes*, p. 148.

8. Alice Miller, *For Your Own Good: Hidden Cruelty in Child-Rearing and the Roots of Violence*, tr. Hildegarde and Hunter Hannum (New York: Farrar, Straus & Giroux, 1983), p. 106.

9. Miller, *Drama*, p. xv.

10. Ibid, p. 7.

11. Froma Walsh, "Reconsidering Gender in the Marital Quid pro Quo," in Monica McGoldrick, Carol M. Anderson, and Froma Walsh, eds. *Women in Families: A Framework for Family Therapy* (New York: W. W. Norton, 1989), p. 273.

12. Diane P. Holder and Carol M. Anderson, "Women, Work and the Family," Ibid., p. 368. They refer to a study by J. Portner, "Work and Family: Achieving a Balance," in *Stress and the Family I: Coping with Normative Transitions*, Hamilton I. McCubbin and Charles R. Figley, eds. (New York: Brunner/Mazel, 1983).

13. Nancy Chodorow, *The Reproduction of Mothering: Psychoanalysis and the Sociology of Gender* (Berkeley, Calif.: University of California Press, 1978).

14. For a psychological explanation of the message mothers convey to daughters that they must look to a man but not expect a man to help or understand, see Luise Eichenbaum and Susie Orbach, "The Construction of Femininity," ch. 2 in *Un-*

derstanding Women: A Feminist Psychoanalytic Approach, (New York: Basic Books, 1983).

Chapter 2

1. Madonna Kolbenschlag, *Lost in the Land of Oz: Our Myths, Our Stories and the Search for Identity and Community in American Life* (San Francisco: Harper & Row, 1988), p. 136.

2. Ana-Maria Rizzuto, *The Birth of the Living God: A Psychoanalytic Study* (Chicago: University of Chicago Press, 1979).

3. Ibid., p. 190.

4. Ibid., p. 44ff. Rizzuto designed both a "God questionnaire" and a "family questionnaire" which wonderfully demonstrate the interrelationships between parent and sibling images or *imagos* and God *imagos*.

5. Ibid., p. 45.

6. Charlene Spretnak, ed., *The Politics of Women's Spirituality: Essays on the Rise of Spiritual Power within the Feminist Movement* (New York: Doubleday & Co., Anchor Books, 1982); Marija Gimbustas, "Women and Culture in Goddess-Oriented Old Europe," in Judith Plaskow and Carol P. Christ, *Weaving the Visions: New Patterns in Feminist Spirituality* (San Francisco: Harper & Row, 1989) (also in Spretnak); Gerda Lerner, *The Creation of Patriarchy* (New York: Oxford University Press, 1986); Carol P. Christ, *Laughter of Aphrodite: Reflections on a Journey to the Goddess* (San Francisco: Harper & Row, 1987); Judy Chicago, *The Dinner Party: A Symbol of Our Heritage* (New York: Doubleday, 1979); Elinor W. Gadon, *The Once and Future Goddess: A Symbol for Our Time* (San Francisco: Harper & Row, 1989), and many others.

7. See Marija Gimbustas, "Women and Culture in Goddess-Oriented Old Europe," as well as the introduction by Charlene Spretnak, in Spretnak, *Politics*.

8. Spretnak, *Politics*, p. xii.

9. Lerner, *Patriarchy*, p. 49.

10. Ibid., p. 30.

11. Ibid., p. 78.

12. Ibid., p. 10.

13. Ibid., p. 160. See also Gadon, *Once and Future*, pp. xii, 185.

14. Lerner, *Patriarchy*, p. 181.

15. Sallie McFague, *Models of God: Theology for an Ecological, Nuclear Age* (Philadelphia: Fortress Press, 1987), p.33. The

book received an American Academy of Religion award for excellence.

16. For a recent discussion of God language in the New Testament, see Robin D. Mattison, "God/Father: Tradition and Interpretation," *Reformed Review* 42 (Spring 1989): 189–206.

17. Rosemary Radford Ruether, *Sexism and God-Talk: Toward a Feminist Theology* (Boston: Beacon Press, 1983), p. 66.

18. Riane Eisler, *The Chalice and the Blade: Our History, Our Future* (San Francisco, Harper & Row, 1987), pp. 20–21.

19. In Brown and Bohn, *Christianity, Patriarchy and Abuse*, pp. 1–30.

20. Ibid., p. 2.

21. Brock, *Journeys*, pp. 52–53.

22. I am grateful to Jenny Yates Hammett for this insight. See Jenny Yates Hammett, *Woman's Transformations: A Psychological Theology* (Lewiston, N.Y.: Edwin Mellen Press, 1982), p. 57. She reminds her reader that the Hebrew word for Spirit, *ruach*, is feminine.

23. Christ, *Laughter*, p. 21. This is the reworking of a story which Elie Wiesel tells in which God and man change places.

24. Starhawk, "Witchcraft as Goddess Religion," in Spretnak, *Politics*, p. 51.

25. McFague, *Models*.

26. John Calvin, *Calvin: Institutes of the Christian Religion*, ed. John T. McNeill. (Philadelphia: Westminster Press, 1960), pp. 35, 37.

Chapter 3

1. Kolbenschlag, *Oz*, p. 137.

2. Erik Erikson, *Childhood and Society*, 2nd ed., rev. & enl. (New York: W. W. Norton, 1963).

3. Abraham Maslow, *Toward A Psychology of Being* (Princeton, N.J.: Van Nostrand, 1962), p. 152.

4. For a detailed elaboration of the components of self esteem, see chapter 3 in Linda Tschirart Sanford and Mary Ellen Donovan, *Women and Self-Esteem* (New York: Doubleday & Co., Anchor Books, 1984); see also the earlier work by Stanley Coopersmith, *The Antecedents of Self-Esteem* (San Francisco: W. H. Freeman, 1967).

5. Jackson, *Self-Esteem*.

6. See Kim Chernin, *The Obsession: Reflections on the Tyranny of Slenderness* (New York: Harper & Row, 1981); Susan C. Wooley and Orland W. Wooley, "Eating Disorders: Obesity

and Anorexia," in Annette M. Brodsky and Rachel Hare-Mustin, *Women and Psychotherapy: An Assessment of Research and Practice* (New York: Guilford, 1980); and Eichenbaum and Orbach, *Understanding Women*, pp. 169–174.

7. Jean Baker Miller, *Toward a New Psychology of Women* (Boston: Beacon Press, 1976), p. 94.

8. See Mary E. Hunt, "Defining Women-Church," *Waterwheel: A Quarterly Newsletter of the Women's Alliance for Theology, Ethics, and Ritual* 3, no. 2 (Summer 1990): 1; and Rosemary Radford Ruether, *Women-Church: Theology and Practice of Feminist Liturgical Communities* (San Francisco: Harper and Row, 1985). Women-Church is also discussed in the next chapter of this book.

9. Miriam Greenspan suggests that "without an adequate conception of how motherhood is shaped by the patriarchal rule of the father in the family, the extent of a mother's power over her children is both wildly overestimated and severely misunderstood." In other words, mother is not the all-powerful figure children see her to be but an oppressed woman held accountable for major social responsibilities that ought to be shared by parents who are co-equals in all aspects of family and social life. Miriam Greenspan, *A New Approach to Women and Therapy* (New York, McGraw-Hill, 1983), p.18.

10. Brock, *Journeys*, p. 22.

11. See Anne Wilson Schaef's books, *Co-Dependence: Misunderstood—Mistreated*, (Minneapolis: Winston Press, 1986), and *When Society Becomes An Addict*, (New York: Harper & Row, 1987); also Melody Beattie, *Codependent No More: How to Stop Controlling Others and Start Caring for Yourself* (Center City, Minn.: Hazelden, 1987). While I appreciate many of the insights in these books, I am uncomfortable with the "addiction" label that Schaef especially seems to apply almost everywhere. I do not think that either Schaef or Beattie place enough value on dependency as a legitimate quality of mutual relationship.

12. A study of upper-elementary school children's self esteem concluded that self esteem is for girls more than boys related to perceived capacities to do schoolwork. Linda J. Alpert-Gillis and James P. Connell, "Gender and Sex-Role Influences on Children's Self-Esteem," *Journal of Personality* 57, no. 1 (March 1989): 97–114.

13. See Erik Erikson, *Childhood and Society*, 2nd ed., rev. & enl. (New York: W. W. Norton, 1963).

14. Daniel J. Levinson includes the Dream as part of the structure of men's lives in a study, Levinson et al., *The Seasons of a Man's Life* (New York: Alfred A. Knopf, 1978); see also James W. Fowler on vocation in *Becoming Adult, Becoming Christian: Adult Development and Christian Faith* (San Francisco: Harper & Row, 1984).

15. Marci McCaulay, Laurie Mintz, and Audrey A. Glen, "Body Image, Self-Esteem and Depression Proneness: Closing the Gender Gap," *Sex Roles: A Journal of Research* 18, nos. 7/8 (1988): 381–391. The study was based on the population of a small, private liberal-arts college.

16. Lisa R. Silberstein, Ruth H. Striegel-Moor, Christine Timko, and Judith Rodin, "Behavioral and Psychological Implications of Body Dissatisfaction: Do Men and Women Differ?" *Sex Roles* 19, nos. 3/4 (1988): 219–232. The study was based on responses from 45 female and 47 male Yale University undergraduates.

Chapter 4

1. Winnicott, *Maturational Processes*, p. 133.

2. Polly Young-Eisendrath and Florence L. Wiedemann, *Female Authority: Empowering Women Through Psychotherapy* (New York: Guilford, 1987), p. 31.

3. For a development of this theme, see chapter 8, "Serving Others' Needs," in Miller, *Toward a New Psychology*.

4. National Coalition Against Domestic Violence, 1012 14th Street, NW, Washington, D.C. 20005.

5. Greenspan, *A New Approach*, p. 214.

6. The Cornell study headed by Julianne Imperato-McGinley, involves work done in the early 1970s by Jo Durden-Smith and Diane de Simone. Reported in John Shelby Spong, *Living in Sin? A Bishop Rethinks Human Sexuality* (San Francisco: Harper & Row, 1988).

7. For a full explanation of Bowen theory see Michael E. Kerr and Murray Bowen, *Family Evaluation: An Approach Based on Bowen Theory* (New York: W. W. Norton, 1988).

Chapter 5

1. Jean Baker Miller, M.D., *Toward a New Psychology of Women*, 2nd ed. (Boston: Beacon Press, 1986), p. xv.

2. Bednar, Wells, and Peterson, *Self-Esteem*, p. 81, n. 83.

3. Ibid., p. 74.

4. Nelle Morton, *The Journey Is Home* (Boston: Beacon Press, 1985).

5. I owe this insight to my student, research assistant, colleague, and friend, Betsy Halsey.

6. Sharon Hicks and Carol M. Anderson, "Women on Their Own," in *Women in Families*, ed. McGoldrick, Anderson, and Walsh, p. 311.

7. Ibid., p. 321. The authors refer to the work of E. Rothblum and V. Franks, "Custom Fitted Straight Jackets: Perspectives on Women's Mental Health," in *The Trapped Woman: Catch-22 in Deviance and Control*, ed. Josefina Figueira-McDonough and Rosemary Sarri (Newbury Park, Calif.: Sage Publications, 1987).

8. L. Radloff, "Sex Differences in Depression: The Effects of Occupation and Marital Status," *Sex Roles* 1 (1975): 249–269. Cited in Myrna M. Weissman, "Depression," in Brodsky and Hare-Mustin, *Women and Psychotherapy*, p. 102.

9. Greenspan, *A New Approach*, p. 205.

10. See Miller, *Toward a New Psychology* (1976); Carol Gilligan, *In A Different Voice: Psychological Theory and Women's Development* (Cambridge, Mass.: Harvard University Press, 1982); Carol E. Franz and Kathleen M. White, "Individuation and attachment in personality development: Extending Erikson's theory," in *Gender and Personality: Current Perspectives on Theory and Research*, ed. Abigail J. Stewart and Brinton M. Lykes (Durham, N.C.: Duke University Press, 1985), pp. 136–168.

11. I am grateful to Merle R. Jordan for his insight into the false God/false self covenant. See *Taking on the Gods: The Task of the Pastoral Counselor* (Nashville: Abingdon, 1986), p. 30.

12. The following suggestions appear in my article "Faith and Self-Esteem," *The Journal of Pastoral Care* 42, no. 2 (Summer 1988): 125–137.

13. Works like Carolyn Bohler, *Prayer on Wings: A Search for Authentic Prayer* (San Diego: LuraMedia, 1990); Brock, *Journeys*; Brown and Bohn, *Christianity, Patriarchy, and Abuse*; Joann Wolski Conn, ed., *Women's Spirituality: Resources for Christian Development* (Mahwah, N.J.: Paulist Press, 1986); Mary E. Hunt, *Fierce Tenderness: Toward a Feminist Theology of Friendship* (Crossroad, 1990); McFague, *Models*; Plaskow and Christ, *Weaving the Visions*; and Spretnak, *Politics* are but a few of many titles available to women who seek feminist material for their spiritual renewal.

14. Miller, *Drama*, p. xv.

Index